London's Underground Suburbs

Dennis Edwards

Capital Transport

First published 1986
Second edition 2003

Published by Capital Transport Publishing
38 Long Elmes, Harrow Weald, Middlesex

Printed by CS Graphics, Singapore

This book is dedicated to the late Ron Pigram who gave encouragement and help for the first edition

Acknowledgements

Roger Brasier, Alan A. Jackson and Peter Nichols for reading the draft.
Clive Smith and David Smith for help with photographs.

Photographic credits

London's Transport Museum	1, 3, 6, 16, 19, 21, 23, 24 (left), 33 (top), 35, 38, 39 (bottom), 40/41, 43, 44, 45, 46, 47 (top), 59, 62/63, 65 (bottom), 69, 73, 75, 77 (bottom), 80, 81 (top), 85, 90, 94, 104 (top) 107 (top)
Commercial postcards	4, 9, 10, 11, 13, 15, 17, 20, 24/25, 26, 27 (both), 28, 29, 31, 36, 37 (top), 53, 55 (bottom), 65 (top), 67, 70, 78, 81 (bottom), 82, 83, 86, 87, 89, 92, 93 (bottom), 95, 97, 99, 103, 105, 107 (bottom)
Aerofilms Ltd	33 (main), 37 (bottom), 47 (bottom)
Peter Bancroft collection	112
Dennis Edwards collection	12, 49, 50, 51, 52, 55 (top), 56 (top), 71, 77 (top), 101, 102, 106
Charles F. Klapper	79 (top), 91
London Borough of Hillingdon	49 (top)
Odeon Cinemas	60/61

The first edition of this book was published by Baton.

Title Page **Golders Green station before the extension of the line to Edgware.**

CONTENTS

INTRODUCTION

A multitude with spades and axes armed
To lay hills plain, fell woods, or valleys fill,
Or where plain raise hill, or over-lay
With bridge rivers proud . . .
　　　　　Milton, Paradise Regained, Book III

The expansion of London in the first years of the twentieth century was one of the most remarkable events of recent history. Heady with England's prosperity as the last golden flickers of sunlight fell upon that Victorian age of achievement, the great City continued to draw more and more people into itself. Slowly at first during Edwardian days, but then with increasing pressure, house building was undertaken in the immediate north and west London suburbs as this vast press of humanity struggled to improve its lot. South London had already grown, but by the 1920s, as the men returned home from the Great War in search of the country 'fit for heroes to live in', there emerged a growing awareness that their lives should alter in keeping with the new age. Everyone ought at least to have a roof over their head. And this undercurrent of social unease with the housing conditions of central London became so strong that the urge to have a home in the new suburbs became the major event of the time. By a curious paradox, it all took place during the time of great economic depression.

There were many forces at work. One of the strongest was the expansion of London's Underground railway system by men like Lord Ashfield and Frank Pick, who were aggressively looking for more profitability from their public transport services.

After the First World War the tube lines were pushed out from London into open fields, with complete assurance that the developers and builders would quickly cover every piece of nearby land with houses. Soon there was to be no stop to the housing momentum; there appeared to be endless green fields, and always a multitude of young couples who sought to move out of smog-prone and fly-infested London into the home of their dreams.

Vast new housing estates spread out; newspaper advertisements insistently offered houses for tiny deposits. Many more families could afford to buy for the price of the rent they were paying each week. The media said that everything was suddenly possible; it was a brave new world populated with babies, mortgages and, of course, Mr Pick's smart new Underground trains.

Let us relax and take a look back over those days. First, you must imagine the spirit and feel of those times – of fly-papers, meat safes, the heavy whirl of tram motors, and grocers' shops where most items were sold loose and therefore had to be weighed. Sugar, for example, was customarily poured into a dark blue bag while you waited. It was a time of popping motor-cycles, but few cars and no television. Wireless sets and wind-up gramophones were the 'must have' icons for those who could afford them. It was a musical era. The latest sounds of Roy Fox would issue from the gramophone. The dining-room clock, on the mantelpiece above the new tiled Aztec fireplace, would sound each quarter hour with its 'Westminster' chimes. A packet of Abdulla cigarettes would be lying on the coffee table beside a bronze statuette of a naked lady who would produce a light when pressed. Perhaps there would be time for a Green Goddess in one of those modern tall-stemmed cocktail glasses over there . . .

Left **South Ealing District Railway opened in May 1883. The parade of shops is typical of the late Victorian suburbs of this time. The station was reconstructed twice in later times.**

1
GRASS ROUTES
1900–1914

In the autumn of 1900, two men drove in a hansom cab over the lofty heights of Hampstead Heath, high over London. From time to time the driver drew in the reins, allowing the men to leave and walk over the open spaces. Barely a rooftop could be seen. Later they took the cab down to see the level fields north of the hill. The only feature here was an isolated crossroads, fringed by a couple of old houses and some farm buildings. They had reached the rural hamlet of Golders Green.

The men were Harley Hugh Dalrymple Hay (later knighted) and an agent called Lauderbeck, acting for Charles Tyson Yerkes. Yerkes was a financier from Chicago and had been described by the Press of the day as 'the projector of the new Charing Cross, Euston and Hampstead Electric Underground'. His financial backing for the half-completed tube railways of London, as well as his support for the District Railway, resulted in the formation of a parent company on 9th April 1902 – the Underground Electric Railways Company of London Ltd.

The two men in the cab stopped by Golders Green crossroads, and Lauderbeck told Dalrymple Hay that this was the place where the proposed terminus for the railway should be sited. At first Dalrymple Hay was not impressed. There did not seem to be any houses in sight. But his companion pointed out that back in the United States, when railways were built, 'the people followed'. When plans were completed for the new tube, Yerkes himself took the same cab journey, accompanied by his Vice Chairman, H.C. Davis. When they reached the top of the Heath by the famous 'Jack Straw's Castle', the heavy rain through which they passed gave way to sun, and Davis showed Yerkes the gleaming spires and towers of London. The scene impressed Yerkes: 'Davis, I'll make this railway' he said.

On another occasion, Yerkes talked of his ambition 'to convey all London about in tunnels, and that a generation hence London would be completely transformed, so that some people would think nothing of living 20 or more miles from Town owing to these electric railways'. Later, at an Enquiry on the Bill for the Golders Green extension, it was said that 'although Golders Green is but a short distance along the Finchley Road from the populous part of St John's Wood, . . . it is absolutely open country, for the simple reason that there is no means of getting to it'.

The extension was authorised under an Act of 18th November 1902, despite the protests of Hampstead people who considered that the tube tunnels under the Heath would act as a drain, so that all moisture would be led away and that the trees and grass would die. However, the residents did win one big concession: there would be no station between Hampstead and Golders Green. As the Underground felt that this decision would eventually be overruled, work started on the platforms of an intermediate station near The Bull & Bush – the famous public house that was immortalised in the music hall song by Florrie Forde. But the shafts from the surface were never sunk, nor any buildings erected. The platforms remain unused to this day, although the space was used for secure storage of London Transport documents during the Second World War.

Work on the line began in September 1903 and was completed in December 1905, but much remained to be done before the trains could start running. Land was cleared at Golders Green for the depot and station. Yerkes never lived to see the public opening. He died at the Waldorf Astoria Hotel, New York, on 29th September 1905.

The Extension to Metro-land.

Of course, the Hampstead tube was not the first London Underground railway to reach the country-side. The original Underground line – the Metropolitan Railway – had extended out into the Middlesex countryside and beyond to the Chilterns in the 1880s and 1890s, as part of Sir Edward Watkin's grandiose scheme to provide a route for his Great Central Railway Company (then the Manchester, Sheffield & Lincolnshire) to London, the South Coast and thence perhaps by a Channel tunnel to Paris!

The original forerunner of the Metropolitan Railway's country extensions was the single track Metropolitan & St John's Wood Railway, which was opened as far as Swiss Cottage on the 13th April 1868. The line was doubled in the 1870s, and was extended via Finchley Road to West Hampstead in 1879. Originally the St John's Wood promoters had planned to build their line up to Hampstead, but the railway was absorbed into the Metropolitan, and the route was to lead into another direction.

West Hampstead in 1879 was still a semi-rural place. Indeed, so lonely and quiet was it that people were afraid to walk along West End Lane at night because of the dense hedges and overhanging trees. Yet, within a few years, the entire area would be covered by rows of tall terraced houses, with hardly an open space anywhere.

Kilburn had been known in the 18th century as Kilburn Wells, attracting the gentry and their ladies out from Georgian London. The Metropolitan Railway was extended beyond Kilburn to Harrow in 1880. An early railway guide book said that 'amongst the charms of Kilburn is its proximity to the countryside' – a claim that even by 1890 would be hard to justify! Willesden Green was opened on the 24th November 1879. 'Although at present there are so few houses in this locality, buildings are in course of formation and, no doubt, considering the desirability of the site and its easy communication with London, many more will follow: villas and houses to rent from £70 to £200 p.a,' the guide book predicted.

All the fields along the Edgware Road and south of the Metropolitan line rapidly filled up with street after street of housing, the spread eventually stretching as far north as Cricklewood. When the Metropolitan reached Harrow, the land between the station at the foot of the famous Hill and the London & North Western line at Harrow & Wealdstone was soon built upon, absorbing the hamlet of Greenhill.

But it was at Northwood, a remote hamlet on the borders of Middlesex and Hertfordshire, that an attempt was made to introduce a satellite suburb. The station was opened on the 1st September 1887, but the new paint and bright gravel approaches initially attracted only a handful of travellers. Indeed, so few passengers arrived in the early weeks that *The Times* reporter, who braved the long journey from Baker Street, said that the line was doomed to failure.

However, anticipating the possibility that the new line might bring in house buyers, David Carnegie JP put his Eastbury estate on the market on the 25th March 1887. The estate was bought by Murray Maxwell Hallowell Carew, the son of an Admiral who had served as one of Nelson's captains. Carew offered building plots in 52 lots at his first sale. 'A rare opportunity for small capitalists and speculators to invest,' said *The Watford Observer*. Carew specified that the houses to be erected in Maxwell and Murray Roads should cost at least £750. At the other end of the social scale, he offered plots for the erection of cottages in High Street costing no less than £120. A further ten land sales were held in the next few years, and the roads were named after him and members of his family.

Unique among railways, the Metropolitan was empowered to issue building licences and lease its land to developers. The Metropolitan Railway Surplus Lands stock was separated from the railway stock under a separate Committee from 1st July 1887. The Surplus Lands Committee promoted a number of estates including Cecil Park, Pinner, the earliest houses on this estate dating from 1900.

Right **Willesden Green old station opened on 24th November 1879. The station was rebuilt in a more imposing style just before the First World War.**

In pre-electric days between West Hampstead and Willesden Green. The tracks of the Great Central Railway are those nearest the camera. The Beyer Peacock locomotive is number 34, later sold to Bradford Corporation. The houses under construction in the background are along Dartmouth Road c1908 and could be rented for £70 pa. The builder's publicity of the time stated: 'The houses now being constructed are of singular convenience and, as to style, expertly tailored'.

Station Approach, Willesden Green.

Kilburn High Road – A typical inner London shopping street in Edwardian days. The Metropolitan station opened on the 24th November 1879. This parade of shops at the junction with Iverson Road is still there today. A third bridge was added in 1914–15 in conjunction with the widening of the Metropolitan Railway.

Houses in Dollis Hill/ Dudding Hill area, c1908. The developer was J C Hill & Co of Archway. They had an estate office conveniently sited in one of their new houses at 2 Burnley Road, near to the new Dollis Hill station. The houses were a more opulent version of the traditional tunnel-back terraced houses. A down deposit of £10 was required, and the ground rent was £6 pa. Repayments were calculated at 10s 7d (53p) per week for 15 years. Houses of this type now sell at well over £350,000.

10

Beyond Neasden, where the Metropolitan Railway works were established in 1882 and included a workers' village, the real countryside began. The first Wembley Park station opened on 12th May 1894, and one of the first trains to call there is said to have been a football special. Football was only one of many sports available in the attractive grounds of the park which had been acquired from the Grey family in the late 1870s by the Metropolitan Railway in conjunction with the line's extension to Harrow. This photograph is from 1902.

The Lodge, Park Lane, Wembley Park, a century ago. A sign (left) directs walkers through the delightful grounds to Wembley Park station. Incredibly this lodge still exists, incorporated into a modern house at the busy junction of Wembley Park Drive, Park Lane and Wembley Hill Road.

The Lodge, Wembley.

Watkin's Folly seen through the mist during the building of the Great Central Railway from Neasden to Northolt Junction (South Ruislip), 1904. The beginning of Edwardian housing development on the slopes of Wembley Hill can also be seen. The Tower closed in 1902, when the lifts failed. The rusty frame of the Tower remained until 1908. The site was later occupied by Wembley Stadium.

This is a typical programme of events a year before the opening of the first (and only) stage of the Wembley Tower.

THE MANSION, BARHAM PARK, WEMBLEY.

Pre-suburban Middlesex had many small country estates that were later broken up to form housing developments or public parks. This is Barham Park (formerly Sudbury Lodge), a few minutes' walk from Sudbury Town station (opened by the District Railway on 28th June 1903). The house was owned by George Titus Barham (1860–1937). His father, Sir George Barham (1836–1913) was the founder of the Express Dairy Company in 1864. The house seen here was demolished in 1956–57 despite much local protest; but part of the buildings, Crab House, remains today as a community centre, whilst the park has attractive gardens enjoyed by all.

STATION ROAD, GREENHILL HARROW.

Almost as soon as the Metropolitan Railway station was opened at Harrow-on-the-Hill in August 1880, development of the land between the station and the LNWR station at Harrow & Wealdstone began. The hamlet of Greenhill was soon transformed into roads of large red brick villas. This is Station Road at the junction of St Ann's Road in about 1905. The gardens of the houses on the right were later built over for single storey shops (known as 'bungalow fronts').

Cecil Park Estate,

PINNER.

(The property of the Metropolitan Railway Surplus Lands Committee.)

Rent, £50 or £55.

GOOD CLASS SEMI-DETACHED HOUSES to be LET.   Rents from £50 to £75.

PLOTS OF LAND

for the erection of Houses of good class are also to be let on Building Lease at moderate ground rents.

THIS ESTATE

is beautifully timbered, charmingly situated, and is within a few minutes walk of Pinner Village and of the Metropolitan Railway Station.

The formation of the Metropolitan Surplus Lands Committee in 1887 served to develop housing on land adjacent to the route of the line outwards from Willesden Green. The Cecil Park estate was one of the first ventures into the deep Middlesex countryside. The new residents had their own entrance to the nearby railway station.

Upper right **Perfect Metro-land Houses behind the elms in Paines Lane, Pinner, c1914.** In summer the long back gardens echoed to the sound of tennis balls and the gentle chink of bone china tea cups. In one of the houses on the left the eccentric cartoonist Heath Robinson died on the 13th September 1944.

Lower right **Northwood (in ancient times the northern part of the large rural parish of Ruislip)** was one of the earliest suburban developments of pre-1914 Metro-land. The station opened on the 1st September 1887, and it was the enterprise of the grandly named Murray Maxwell Hallowell Carew who, having bought the Eastbury House estate, placed it on the map. This is Green Lane about fifteen years after the arrival of the Metropolitan. Further shops were added on the left side of the road in 1911.

The Harrow and Uxbridge Railway.

It was the opening of the Harrow and Uxbridge Railway in 1904 that was to be the stimulus to suburban growth in the area which came to be called Metro-land. At the official opening lunch held in a vast marquee erected in the station yard at Uxbridge on the 30th June in that year, the Metropolitan's Chairman had predicted: 'Some of those persons here today will no doubt live to see the districts through which the new line passes develop and furnish homes for London's ever-expanding population', whilst the local press on that day described the village of Ruislip (then the only intermediate station on the line) as 'the sleepy hollow whose character will be gone, and the districts thus opened up will gradually take on the form of charming London suburbs'.

The first housing developments along the new railway were at Ruislip. Under the Town & Country Planning Act of 1909 the Ruislip-Northwood Urban District Council held a competition for the planning of a garden city between Northwood and the area now known as South Ruislip. It called for an ambitious approach, and the first prize was won by Westminster architects A & J Soutar. Their grand boulevard, landscaped Ruislip Reservoir and integrated groups of cottages, shops and villas won great acclaim at an exhibition held in London.

'Ruislip-Northwood has placed the whole country under an obligation by being the first small authority to complete a town planning scheme', said one newspaper. A company called Ruislip Manor Ltd was formed, and its prospectus stated: 'Ruislip Manor Limited aims at introducing all classes into the community . . . but it is not intended to indiscriminately mix all classes together, however'. A few houses were completed before the First World War, but the original project was never revived, although the route of some of the principal roads was kept, and the Council maintained its high standards of planning control. The Ruislip that was eventually to emerge was a very different place from the dreams of 1909. The Council was greatly concerned with the activities of a number of land developers who bought land near the Metropolitan railway in the 1900s. The British Freehold Land Company sold plots for £3 down and 10s 0d (50p) per week, but buyers had to find their own architect and builder. As a result, they often dispensed with the services of an architect and designed their own homes, with disastrous results.

It was a common practice, too, in other areas, even after the First World War. The British Freehold Land Company tempted small investors: 'Try to own a suburban home; it will make you a better citizen and will help your family. The suburbs have fresh air, sunlight, roomy houses, green lawns and social advantages'.

Other local Councils followed the Ruislip example, and the Middlesex suburbs that were to grow a generation later were of brick houses with proper services and usually, although not necessarily, made-up roads. London's Underground suburbs were thus spared the shanty-town type sprawl that was to be the hallmark of many large cities in the United States.

In 1915 the Metropolitan Railway published the first of the famous series of Metro-land guides (although it had published earlier railway guide books). In the very first issue, the Editor wrote: 'The strains which the London business or professional man has to endure amongst the turmoil and bustle of town can only be counter-balanced by the quiet restfulness and comfort of a residence in pure air and rural surroundings'.

High Street (Central) Uxbridge.

Rural Ruislip in 1908 outside the then newly opened Poplars Tea Gardens. The villagers are waiting for the runners in the Olympic Marathon of July 1908 who passed through Ruislip on their way to White City. The race had started in Windsor, and the course was via Slough, Uxbridge, Ickenham, Ruislip and Harrow. On the left in this view is elm-lined West End Road (now High Street) which led to the station.

Left High Street, Uxbridge in the early 20th century. The Met reached here in 1904.

Developments West of Hammersmith.

To the west of London, the Metropolitan District Railway (to give it its full name) had reached Hammersmith in 1874, thus competing with its old rival, the Metropolitan Railway, whose station lay just across the street. The District Railway's publicity of the time claimed with some justification that its own station was 'superior in expedition and convenience to the Metropolitan Railway Company's route from Moorgate Street'.

Further west, in just the same way that local business interests had taken the initiative in the Uxbridge area, Hounslow worthies in Victorian days had encouraged the idea of a rail service into London. Nobody liked to be cut off in a small town. The first trains ran between Hounslow and Mill Hill Park (which became Acton Town from March 1910) as early as 1883. The Metropolitan District Railway, eyes cast firmly westwards, bought up this early railway, so giving some local pride in a permanent connection to Mansion House from the local terminus in Hounslow Town. However, in those days, with Ealing a superior residential district which had been served by the District since 1879, Hounslow was too far away from London to attract large-scale development for what we have come to call the 'commuter class'.

Hounslow's last period of importance dated from the days of the highwaymen and the coach links to Bath. Not much had happened since those times, although 1873 had seen the erection of Hounslow Barracks with an infantry regiment in occupation by 1875.

A new station, called Hounslow Barracks, appeared on the Bath Road in July 1884, leaving the original terminus station out on a limb. There had to be a complicated shunting operation to serve both places, and it was no surprise when, less than two years later, Hounslow Town station was abandoned for another new station on the Barracks line. It was called Heston-Hounslow in a cunning attempt to attract custom from the small village of Heston which then lay, hidden by trees, about half an hour's walk away to the north. Hounslow Town, after its closure in March 1886, remained shut until 1903. It reopened for six years, but finally closed in 1909, the site becoming part of the land attached to Hounslow bus garage.

The Metropolitan District Railway also had a short spur line which ran from Earl's Court to West Brompton. Railway expansion was the order of the day, and in March 1880 the line was pushed beyond West Brompton to Putney Bridge. An agreement was reached with the London & South Western Railway for a further extension to Wimbledon, and the main-line company spanned the Thames with a massive bridge that carried District trains to Wimbledon, which had its first District Railway service from June 1889. There was also an agreement with the main-line railway to use the LSWR lines from Studland Road, Hammersmith, to Richmond. A short connecting spur was all that was needed from Hammersmith, allowing yet another town, Richmond, to be plugged into the District in June 1877.

In 1875–1881 London's first true Garden Suburb, Bedford Park, was built near Turnham Green station. The idea came from Jonathan Carr, and some of the best architects of the day were employed: Norman Shaw was responsible for the layout and the design of many of the buildings. One house was the work of C F A Voysey, whose designs were to have a lasting influence on the villas and houses in the better class Underground suburbs. Norman Shaw and his acolytes fashioned houses which had to be 'in the right place for people of the right type' in a Queen Anne style. It was very much a creation for the rich and upper middle class, with rents from £40 pa.

Here, in Bedford Park, were a church, an inn (The Tabard) and a store, so that residents should want for little other mortal comfort, as well as 'institutes for socal life', since at the time the Garden Suburb was considered to be rather remote from the hurly-burly of fashionable London life. Bedford Park was very advanced for its day and received criticism for its departure from the norm, it being alleged that it was 'the suburb for the artistic bourgeoisie', a view that we may, with the advantage of another age, tend to agree with. A resident told one of the weekly magazine reporters of the time that he felt he was living in some water colour painting of the rural romantic school! The Bedford Park estate remains largely intact today and is well worth a visit for those with an interest in architecture.

Everybody had a garden and for a time the estate produced its own newspaper. Houses also quickly filled the flat fields between Kew Gardens and the railway towards Richmond. Market gardens at Gunnersbury gave way to residential development.

Along the Wimbledon line things were happening fast. By 1895 H S Vaughan in 'The Way about Middlesex' wrote: '*Twenty years ago there was a pleasant country road from Walham Green, bordered by fields, market gardens and nurseries, and grounds with many fruit trees*'. He was writing amid a sea of new houses. The District's extensions into south-west London were said to have brought 'health and betterment to the inhabitants of London'.

Houses 'like several battalions of a gigantic army, marching and counter-marching' were spreading over the south Middlesex fields. By the end of the 19th century most of the land between West Brompton, Hammersmith and Chiswick was developed, and Ealing was already earning its title as the Queen of the Western Suburbs. The steam trains and their uncomfortable carriages were becoming an embarrassment to the District Railway and were soon to be discarded.

The District Railway came under Yerkes' control in 1901; but before that the Ealing & South Harrow Railway had been incorporated in 1894 as part of the District's ambitions to reach Uxbridge. The line was constructed in 1899, but no trains ran on this extension until the pioneer electrification of 1903 between Mill Hill Park (Acton Town) and Park Royal for the Royal Agricultural Society's show. Heavy rains had caused some earth slips farther north, and it was not until the 28th June 1903 that trains could operate to South Harrow. Sidings were laid down for the new electric trains which looked very American in design.

The Metropolitan Railway's Harrow & Uxbridge railway had been built partly on a viaduct to South Harrow from Rayners Lane; but there were no regular passenger trains to connect the two lines until the District Railway began its service to Uxbridge in 1910. It was this rather quiet branch line, through Alperton and Sudbury to South Harrow and rural Rayners Lane, that was to become part of the Piccadilly line's westward extension in 1932–1933, of which more later.

Healthy living on the Hounslow Line about 1910. The poster shows views of Osterley Park, as well as some of the then new houses being erected at nearby areas, such as Spring Grove.

Spring Bridge Road, Ealing Broadway.

Development of Ealing began in the middle of the 19th century, and early commuters used the Great Western Railway into Paddington. By way of improvement a service was later introduced with through trains to the City from Ealing Broadway using the tracks of the Metropolitan Railway for the journey beyond Paddington. The District Railway reached Ealing on 1st July 1879.

A scene from Edwardian days of Spring Bridge Road, not far from the busy Ealing Broadway. Here were small shops selling everything from confectionery (A. J. Stanley) to building supplies and decorating materials (J. E. Edwards).

Large indicators were a common feature of District Line stations in inner London until quite late in the 20th century and can still be seen today at Earl's Court. This magnificent example is at St James's Park.

Right A rare postcard advertising excursions by District Railway to the Middlesex countryside. A typical special fare was the 6d return from Hammersmith to South Harrow (for The Paddocks Tea Gardens and Retreat). Travellers were informed that there was a ten minute service to Sudbury and South Harrow on Sundays, and a half-hourly service to Ruislip.

Off to spend a day in the country. A well dressed private party boards a District Railway train for South Harrow or Eastcote.

The Hampstead Tube Arrives.

This book began with some early facts about Golders Green and how the hamlet became the first railway suburb of the tube lines.

Trains started operating on Saturday 22nd June 1907, the service being officially opened by the President of the Board of Trade, Lloyd George. The service ran from Charing Cross to either Golders Green or Highgate (the junction for the two northern branches being at Camden Town). Travel on the first day was free, and advertisements all over London announced: '*The last link . . . in the chain of communication . . . of a complete system of underground railway transit which it is believed will not only help to solve the pressing problem of street congestion, but will introduce wide reaching changes in the distribution of population, the location of shopping centres and the travel habits of the people*'.

In the next few years great changes were to come about at the hamlet of Golders Green! Even in the years shortly before the building of the line the local authority, Hendon Urban District Council, had opened a new town hall in the centre of old Hendon village. The famous Golders Green Crematorium (then an extremely novel idea for disposing of the dead) was opened in 1902. Street lamps appeared along the Finchley Road about this time, and two estate agents set up their huts in a field near the proposed terminus in October 1905.

The passing of the Edgware & Hampstead Railway Act of the 18th November 1902 and the Watford & Edgware Railway Act of the same year stimulated speculation that housing development would soon take place. There was an immediate improvement in communications to distant Edgware with the arrival of the Metropolitan Electric Tramways' line in 1906. A further extension of the tramway took place to Canons Park, farther north along the Edgware Road, in October 1907. The tube itself was never to get beyond Edgware.

By October 1905 the first house stood ready for occupation at the corner of Finchley Road and Hoop Lane, Golders Green. In the following year, a visitor to the area commented: '*Within sight of the Golders Green terminus of the Hampstead tube, half-a-dozen estate agents' pavilions may be counted dotted about the fields*'.

After the line opened, the growth of Golders Green was rapid. By the end of 1907, seventy-three houses had been completed. In 1914 the construction of 471 houses was recorded. New roads, such as The Grove, The Drive, Templar's Avenue and Wentworth Road, were built. '*All day long there was a continuous hammering which reminds one of distant thunder,*' wrote the editor of the local newspaper, as the armies of carpenters went about their work.

Not far from Golders Green, Hampstead Garden Suburb was being built under the Hampstead Garden Suburb Act of 1906.

The Suburb was the idea of Dame Henrietta Barnett, being 'a place where the poor shall teach the rich and where the rich, let us hope, shall teach the poor to help themselves'.

A set of rules and objectives was drawn up in the prospectus for the estate. Among them were: '*that persons of all classes of society and standards of income shall be accommodated and that the handicapped be welcomed; the cottages and houses should be limited to an average of eight to an acre; roads are to be 40 feet wide and lined with trees*'.

Noise was to be avoided even to the prohibiting of church, chapel or institute bells. Lower ground rents were to be charged in certain areas 'to enable weekly wage earners to live on the estate' – an early example of affordable housing. The houses were to be so planned 'that none shall spoil each other's outlook or rob its neighbour of beauty'.

The architects of the buildings included Edwin Lutyens, C Cowles, C F A Voysey, Geoffrey Lucas and W Curtis-Green. There were churches and a library. But the roads were too narrow for public transport, and the Suburb's carefully planned atmosphere of 'safety and enclosure' proved too much for the working-class residents who soon abandoned their homes to the middle classes and moved back to the relative chumminess of the inner suburbs. Later the peace of the area was to be broken by the construction, across the northern edge, of the diverted A1 road (Falloden Way) in 1928. Large parts of it remain delightful however and properties that come on the market can certainly be described as 'highly desirable'.

Golders Green on a wintry day in 1906. The sign on the left points the way to the site of the future Hampstead tube station. The house is The Hawthorns, occupied by the offices of Ernest Owers, the estate agent. The hut with the flag is the more modest estate office of Raymond & Crump. The tube was opened on Saturday 22nd June 1907 by the President of the Board of Trade, David Lloyd George. Five years earlier land was changing hands at £200 an acre: now it was fetching £1,000.

Golders Green about 1912. On the far left, by the road, is the brick abutment of what will eventually be the bridge carrying the Hampstead Tube extension to Edgware. On the tracks up in the embankment are tube motor-cars temporarily uncoupled from their trains.

In the early days of the Hampstead tube at Golders Green, the countryside not only of Hampstead but also to the north towards Hendon and Edgware was popular for an outing. Here a horse-drawn bus bound for Hendon, with well dressed passengers on board, is about to set off. On summer weekends a band would play in the station forecourt.

Off to Watford by Bakerloo.

The London & North Western Railway had for years neglected the potential of suburban traffic along its main line out of Euston, and, for a long while, the station at Willesden Junction where the North London Railway crossed over the main line was called 'The Wilderness'. But London expanded through Kilburn and Queen's Park towards Willesden.

The arrival of the Metropolitan Railway to the north of this area also stimulated housing. Queen's Park was laid out as a model of working-class housing, and the actual public park itself was opened on the 5th May 1887 by Sir Reginald Hanson. Beyond Willesden Junction there were scruffy fields, and the once rural surroundings that had been painted earlier in that century by the artist Morland were further spoiled by the building of the LNWR's vast sidings at Stonebridge Park. Yet, in 1875, a development here of sixty or so new villas had been described as ideal homes for City men!

It was the arrival of the Bakerloo line that was to open up this part of London for development. The original Baker Street & Waterloo Railway (the name Bakerloo was coined by the *Evening News* writer 'Quex') opened on Saturday 10th March 1906. A short extension opened from Baker Street to Marylebone on the 27th March 1907 to link with the newly built Great Central. Sir Sam Fay of the Great Central Railway arranged for the tube station simply to be called Great Central.

The line was pushed through to Edgware Road on the 15th June 1907 and to Paddington on the 1st December 1913. Powers were obtained in 1911–12 for an extension from here to the surface and alongside the LNWR line to Queen's Park and beyond.

Labour troubles caused by the First World War delayed the completion, and the new line did not reach Queen's Park until 11th February 1915. In May of that year some Bakerloo trains ran out to Willesden Junction. The LNWR had already laid a pair of additional tracks out as far as Watford Junction, with a loop line round Watford via Bushey and High Street, worked by a steam service from 1913. It was planned that LNWR electric trains would use the tracks, but the original LNWR plan for a terminal loop beneath Euston main line station

had been abandoned in favour of a joint Bakerloo/LNWR electric service beyond Queen's Park, with the LNWR electric trains running to and from the existing Euston and Broad Street stations.

Because of the First World War the LNWR electric trains were not ready. In 1920 the Bakerloo was equipped with rolling stock which was specially built for the long run into the countryside – luggage racks and comfortable seats. The external livery was briefly in the LNWR colours instead of traditional Underground red and cream.

Tube trains began running (weekdays only) between Watford Junction and Elephant & Castle on the 16th April 1917, the longest run of all tube lines at that time – just under 21 miles.

Some housing developments took place at Wembley, Harrow & Wealdstone and Hatch End before the outbreak of the First World War. The Avenue and Nugents Park areas of Hatch End were popular with City men. The stations at Harrow & Wealdstone and Hatch End were partly rebuilt, with booking halls designed by Gerald C Horsley, who had worked for Norman Shaw.

The Bakerloo in Hertfordshire: High Street, Bushey Village, with an open-top bus. The Bakerloo began operations through Bushey & Oxhey station to Watford via Watford High Street in April 1917.

Wealdstone.

The Parade.

Wealdstone gradually developed around the LNWR station in the late nineteenth century. The station was one of the earliest on the outskirts of London. It was opened on the 20th July 1837. There was a small speculative development of villas in 1854. Ambitious plans included the laying out of highways such as Harrow View and Pinner View, but there was no building until the 1880s. The Bakerloo reached Wealdstone in 1917 but the arrival of industry – Kodak in 1891 – and other factories had made Wealdstone more of a working class than a commuter suburb.

The Bakerloo in Hertfordshire: south-bound train between Watford High Street and Bushey in 1919. The Grand Union Canal winds round to the right and passes beneath the arches carrying the LNWR main line to Euston.

The Ealing & Shepherd's Bush Railway.

On the 14th May 1908 the Central London Railway (the original 'Tuppenny Tube') was extended from Shepherd's Bush to Wood Lane to serve the Franco-British Exhibition which opened that year at White City.

Over the next few years the line carried vast crowds to the series of international exhibitions held at White City. Agreement was reached with the Great Western Railway for Central London tube trains to use that company's Ealing & Shepherd's Bush Railway (opened for freight in 1917). The new service began in 1920, supplementing the existing District Railway trains for the greater benefit of the favoured middle class residents of Ealing, the First World War having prevented progress with the project.

View From Concert Hall, Franco-British Exhibition, London, 1908.

Franco-British Exhibition 1908: Palace of British Applied Arts viewed from outside the concert hall.

Franco-British Exhibition 1908. This structure was situated between the Central London Railway station at Shepherd's Bush and the 'Mail Coach' public house. The archway minus the towers and canopy, still stands today.

The spectacular ornate main entrance to the
Exhibition grounds from Wood Lane.

Bridge in Court of Honour, Franco-British Exhibition, London, 1908

VALENTINES SERIES
COPYRIGHT

Franco-British Exhibition: The Court of Honour. Here
visitors could voyage along the artificial waterways by
electric launch. After dark, the Court was illuminated
by 16,000 electric bulbs.

Life in Edwardian London.

Apart from the rather grand pioneer developments along the route of the Metropolitan Railway, most middle and lower middle class Londoners in the Edwardian era lived in districts on the fringe of the central area – places such as Wood Green, Kilburn, Willesden, Finsbury Park and Tooting. The average family rented accommodation or often just a room or two. Few owned property. Mortgages required an assured regular income, which many middle class residents enjoyed, but were not widely available at this time at acceptable low rates of interest.

Most of the Edwardian suburbs consisted of long streets of terraced red or yellow brick houses, with projecting bay windows, mullioned in stone, that overlooked small handkerchief-sized front gardens. The rear of some of the larger houses had a slate-roofed extension covering the kitchen and scullery. Lavatories would more often than not be housed separately in the back yard. Bathrooms had started to appear from 1890 onwards, but such luxuries were reserved for the grander households.

A low wall for the more fortunate, otherwise a straggle of privet, separated the occupants of the house from the noise and dirt of the street, whilst Venetian blinds in a drab fawn or dark green colour uniformly provided privacy at the front of the house. These tunnel-back houses had, at best, a small shadowy rear garden, but more usually a yard. Very often, from a convenient large nail driven into the wall on the rear single-storey extension or back fence, a long zinc bath would be suspended for use by the occupants in front of the kitchen range.

The outside of most houses presented a universally dismal view, for brown paint was the order of the day. It was tidy, did not 'shout' and did not show the dirt so much as other shades. The acid London fogs ate deeply into the lead composition of the paint manufactured at that time. A few brave hearts, who wanted to be 'different', painted their houses black and white, or black and cream. It was regarded by the neighbours as very advanced and 'something to do with the Dutch'.

Within the home, starched lace curtains helped to conceal the hideous Venetian blinds. The parlour or front room was kept for visitors, or for Christmas celebrations. Most people had extended families – it was not unusual for widowed grannies and grand-dads or elderly spinster aunts to live with them – together with several cats and dogs. Walls were dark and varnished, especially on the staircases. Wallpapers were heavily patterned in deeply coloured floral prints.

Yet, despite common belief that things were not much different from Victorian times, the Edwardian home had progressed, with carpets (where possible) and linoleum. Not everybody by any means actually had a kitchen. Some in shared houses had to make do with a gas stove on the half-landing. There would be no aids or machines to speed the household tasks: the kitchen range would have to be raked and polished with 'black lead', the copper lit on washing day (always a Monday!). The washing process would occupy the greater part of the day, with the regular poking of the items in the copper with a 'dolly', followed by the laborious processes of rinsing, 'blueing' and starching items before as much moisture as possible was squeezed out with the aid of a heavy iron mangle. With the first 'cat's whisker' wireless set appearing only in the 1920s, entertainment before that time was very much a home-made affair. A family sing-song around that much desired Victorian status symbol, the parlour piano, was very popular.

During those early years in the Underground suburbs, there was always the local Music Hall for entertainment. Music Halls invariably sported luxurious interiors, lavishly decked in crimson and gold. Frank Matcham, who was also responsible for the decoration of early cinemas, was a leading Music Hall designer of the time.

On summer days the call of 'Appy Ampstead' delighted the children, and it was only a short tube or bus ride away for most people. The newly electrified Metropolitan and District Railways encouraged the desire to spend the day farther afield – to Putney Heath or Richmond perhaps, by the River, or a walk on Wimbledon Common. For middle-class children, it was no longer satisfying to have:

A tuppenny ride on a tramcar
Down to Victoria Park
A tuppenny ride on a donkey
To show I was having a lark.

The City and South London tube station at Clapham Common opened in 1900. Opposite is the Plough public house. Note the central 'slot' between the tram tracks from which the trams picked up electric current.

Hampstead High Street looking towards Holly Hill at the beginning of the Edwardian era. the Hampstead Tube station was later built beyond the row of shops on the right, opposite the old Town Hall and its clock tower.

2
AFTER THE
GREAT WAR

The Call of the Open Air.

The days of the great school treat for a year's good attendance at elementary school or Sunday School were the norm in the Edwardian era and remained highly popular for some decades to come. In West London's inner suburbs, children were taken out on highly organised outings – some financed by local traders – to the countryside at Ruislip or Eastcote. The Pavilion Gardens specially catered for such parties in the 1920s and consisted of a large area at Field End Road, Eastcote, set aside for picnics, rounders, donkey rides and roundabouts. There was cover for over 4,000 people if it started to rain. The Ruislip tea gardens at The Poplars was another favourite, as was The Paddocks at South Harrow.

Open-air life blossomed for adults too, but this was mostly confined to their only spare day – Sunday. Golders Green and Hendon were popular in early days, whilst anglers travelled into Middlesex to streams around Uxbridge or, perhaps, the Kingsbury reservoir, making for the famous old pub, The Welsh Harp, on the Edgware Road to discuss 'the one that got away'. The reservoir itself eventually became known as the Welsh Harp. The new Hampstead tube had to lengthen its Sunday trains from four to six cars during the summer months. At the same time, a rash of new posters appeared, most of them very attractive and carrying the legend 'Book to Hampstead or Golders Green'. There was even a local band which played in the forecourt of Golders Green station to the passing crowds.

The District Railway, which on 22nd July 1909 had started running 'through' trains from Ealing Broadway to Southend-on-Sea, was not to be outdone, and some colourful seaside scenes appeared on its posters. Trains consisted of special sets of London, Tilbury & Southend Railway carriages, which were hauled by electric locomotives as far east as Barking.

All these changes in Londoners' social behaviour were taking place slowly over the years. There was not too much money around for pleasurable outings, but there was a general feeling that it was healthy to get out into the open air whenever possible. A number of activists were urging concern about public living standards. The Boer War had found recruits to have poor physical health, pointing to widespread lack of proper food and living conditions.

Ebenezer Howard with his idealistic dream for Letchworth and his book 'GARDEN CITIES OF TOMORROW' had also given a bold lead in this direction. With constant child loss through diptheria, consumption and scarlet fever – major killer diseases in the 1900s until the Second World War – there was an unconscious unrest about the way that most Londoners were forced to live. Everyone wanted clean country air for their children. 'Overcrowding is dangerous – the air in densely crowded areas becomes germ-laden', Government reports conceded. Just before the outbreak of the First World War the national newspapers were urging better housing and a world where 'the fresh air of the country districts will be available to all . . . where the slums are gone and where modern sanitation excels'.

The new network of Underground railways in combination with the electrification of the Southern Railway after the First World War was to provide some of the answers and to bring a new way of life for millions who could use this mode of transport to separate their work in London from their outlying homes.

In the rough jostle of rush hour on the tube lines, it was the norm for males to offer ladies their seat, although as yet few women took this form of transport to work.

The Underground transforming open country in 1923. The construction of a terminal station at Edgware is in progress and on the left of the picture the building of a parade of shops and a new road has begun. Houses soon followed. In 1927, the Underground advertised 'There is room to live at Edgware . . . In these pleasant rural surroundings new estates are now being laid out. Yet from this rustic retreat London and all its urbanities can be reached in about 30 minutes.'

EDGWARE
FAST TRAINS
EVERY FEW MINUTES
UNDERGROUND

Homes for Heroes.

After the First World War, the slogan 'a land fit for heroes' was on every politician's lips. Men were just not prepared to go back to a life of despair. To own their own home was the dream of most ex-servicemen – not just the middle classes, but the working class men as well.

The Metropolitan Railway seemed to be always ready for any eventuality. The General Manager, Selbie, wrote in 1918: '*In view of the large demand there will be for houses as soon as Peace is declared, and the forces are demobilised . . . I am of the opinion that the scheme of forming an Estate Company (to develop the spare land beside the railway tracks for housing) should be taken in hand forthwith*'.

For north-west London, the result was the Metropolitan Railway Country Estates Ltd, formed in 1919. It had originated 'not merely to provide superior houses in the rural countryside near London, but also to create new passenger traffic'. Here was the early clue to the Railway Company's extreme interest in home development. Very few houses were however built in the early 1920s due to the aftermath of the War, shortages of materials and skilled labour, as well as national exhaustion.

But in a few years things started to move, with the resumption by the Government in 1923 of private subsidies, so that developers could raise the capital to purchase land. The *Architectural Journal* of that day found that 'thanks to private enterprise . . . estates are springing up on the outskirts of London which promise to meet an urgent need'. Middlesex, flat and sparsely populated, attracted many builders. Uxbridge and Hounslow already enjoyed generous public transport facilities. It was here, according to the *Evening News* in 1933, that there was 'a solution for the desire of people to live in more rural surroundings and away from the noise of London traffic'.

In the same year the Middlesex County Officer for Health commented on the influence that the Underground railway was having on the county, enhancing its growth and bringing hitherto inaccessible parts within easy reach of London. 'The builder has followed hard upon the improvement in transport and is rapidly transforming the remaining parts of Middlesex into urban communities.'

Top **The Eastbury Farm Estate at Northwood offered stylish living on the Metropolitan railway for affluent businessmen. E.S. Reid also built Harrow Garden Village at Rayners Lane.**

Above **A bungalow on the Bakerloo; These compact homes were ten minutes from the Bakerloo/LMS station at Kenton. Rapid developments were already covering the last of the open spaces in the area in 1934.**

Because of the growth of the suburbs after 1920, the Church of England was concerned that there should be adequate places of worship. The Bishop of London set out the 'Forty Five Churches Fund' in 1930, the finances coming mainly from the sale of redundant churches in inner London.

A cartoon from a 1929 issue of the Underground Group's staff magazine.

The Edgware Extension.

In the early 1920s the plans for extending the Hampstead tube from Golders Green were revived. Despite some houses having been built over the projected route at Golders Green, parcels of land farther north had already been acquired and fenced by 1913. Much additional expense was, however, incurred with the need to purchase the houses and land at Golders Green and to demolish the houses to make way for the viaduct which was to carry the Underground. In order to save compensation money, sometimes only half of a pair of semi-detached houses was bought, the other half remaining very close to the railway. The extension also included some heavy engineering work just north of Hendon station. The old village of Hendon stands on a hill called The Burroughs, and the new line was carried beneath by twin tube tunnels more than half a mile long.

The LNER terminus at Edgware offered a poor train service to London via Finchley, although there was a fairly busy goods and coal yard. The yard lasted long after the the final passenger steam train (1939) and was not closed until 4th May 1964. The track was removed in September of that year. The old LNER route was to have formed a Northern line extension from Finchley via Mill Hill, but was never completed. Quite a complicated pattern of services between Edgware and central London would have resulted if it had.

The Hampstead tube station at Edgware was designed in a classical Italian style by S A Heaps, and was 'sufficiently dignified to command respect'. Between Golders Green and Edgware were intermediate stations at Brent (originally to have been named Woodstock), Hendon Central, Colindale and Burnt Oak (opened on the 27th October 1924), each having 150ft long island platforms. At Edgware a bus station was laid out in the forecourt. Provision was also made for a further extension into Hertfordshire – Watford was at one stage proposed. The shops opposite Edgware station were built on deep concrete foundation walls, strong enough to form the sides of a short tunnel. The line opened as far as Hendon on the 19th November 1923, when the ceremony was performed by the President of the Board of Trade, Sir Philip Lloyd Grahame, who was MP for Hendon.

The GNR (LNER after 1923) terminus at Edgware opened on the 22nd August 1867. The railway was intended to go on to Bushey and Watford, so two platforms were provided. The stationmaster and his family lived in accommodation above the station. The entrance to the goods yard is on the right. In the 1920s and 1930s the yard was busy with building materials for the new housing estates. A poster advertises excursions to Skegness and Scotland, whilst just to the left of the small building with the chimney is a poster advertising Jones Brothers of Holloway, a popular store with North London folk. In the latter years before its closure in the 1990s it was a branch of the John Lewis Partnership. The station closed to passenger traffic from 11th September 1939, and to goods traffic in 1964.

Facing page top **Edgware at the junction of High Street and Station road in the early 1930s with the newly built parade of shops a few hundred yards from the tube station. A coach on the original Green Line service heads south along the High Street while an LGOC single-deck LT type bus stands outside one of the vacant shop units of the newly erected parade.**

Facing page bottom **Hendon grew rapidly with the extension of the Underground. At the end of the First World War the population was 57,000. By 1931 it was 115,640, and by 1939 approaching 155,000. This 1930 view shows a shopping parade being built around Hendon Central station on the new A41 roundabout.**

LIVE ON THE UNDERGROUND

HENDON

It's not the distance that counts ; *it's the time spent on the journey.* That is the real test of convenience. From Hendon it takes 27½ minutes to the Bank, 23 minutes to Leicester Square. These stations are convenient for business and for pleasure. Alongside the Underground from Hendon to Edgware new estates are now being laid out, with the Hampstead Garden Suburb as exemplar. The terms of house purchase are convenient—you live in the house whilst you pay for it.

The most fastidious parent can find a school at Hendon for his children whatever may be the variety of modern education that he affects. There are eight council schools and seven non-provided schools apart from the unnumbered private and special schools. For hard exercise there are many tennis clubs, and for recreation golf courses at Hendon and Colindale. Make an opportunity to pay a visit of inspection to Hendon. *You can start conveniently from any Underground Station.*

Two Underground press advertisements from the mid-1920s are shown on this page. Both concentrate on time of journey into central London rather than distance.

Why not live at Edgware ?

A country home and a garden surrounded by fields, a few minutes' walk to the Shops and the Tube Station.

30 minutes to Charing Cross. 40 minutes to Bank.

SEASONS		1 Month	3 Months
	Charing Cross . .	23/-	62/6
	Bank . . .	24/6	67/6

UNDERGROUND

The Edgware section opened on Monday, 18th August 1924. Some of the other stations lacked final architectural details for a few weeks. Passing loops were later provided at Brent to enable non-stop trains to be run at peak periods for a time from 13th June 1927.

The extension was a great success. The smart new trains, in Post Office red, with white upper panels and chocolate waistbands, were soon filled with passengers not only from the districts along the line but from places farther afield. Often the feeder bus services brought them from quite some distance to Edgware. Here they could board one of the frequent trains and be in Tottenham Court Road in 35 minutes. By comparison, the LNER steam trains from Edgware took almost an hour to reach King's Cross.

Commenting on the opening, *The Times* of the 17th March 1923 stated: '*The hitherto quiet and purely rural Edgware village is seeing a new and steadily rising level of land values . . . the district presents plenty of opportunities*'. Opportunities, indeed, for the land agents and builders! One of the first on the scene at Edgware was George Cross. He bought seventy acres in October 1919 and made a handsome profit when part was purchased by the Underground for the site of the station and sidings.

Cross was later instrumental in creating the modern Edgware, and many years later he was to recall the thrill obtained in helping to build a new district: '*. . . in moulding that slice of the suburbs of London in any way I pleased; planning roads as I would; naming them as I fancied*'.

Those were the days when planning laws were simple and local councils seldom intervened. One of the earliest large-scale developments was at Burnt Oak, where the London County Council laid out the vast Watling estate from 1926.

By 1925, Hendon and Edgware were spreading over the hills and fields at a speed that amazed visitors. One writer in a feature on new houses around London wrote: '*Within the last two or three years a considerable change has taken place, and a beautiful garden suburb has sprung up at Edgware. Handsome shops are already erected, and good wide roads have been constructed, or are in course of construction*'. Soon the London newspapers were bristling with advertisements for houses alongside the new railway. H Sousley announced his Deans Lane estate, Edgware, by encouraging inner suburban dwellers to come out to Edgware's green fields with his slogan 'No more Landlords'. But he was selective when it came to the people whom he wanted on his estates: 'Strictly satisfactory references required . . . weekly repayment 35/-' (£1.75).

The Underground posters showed a row of Victorian terraced houses and the headlines: 'Leave this and move to Edgware'. Later posters asked: '*Edgware . . . live there. Live where? Edgware!*'

The newspapers were full of advertisements for Haymills estates at Hendon, with architecturally-designed houses by Herbert Welch. 'Hendon is one of the prettiest of the residential places to live . . . and for residential purposes it is enhanced by a first-class railway service.'

The Raymond family had been dairy farmers at Golders Green in Victorian days. Leslie Raymond set up as an estate agent with his brothers, George and Frank.

A LITTLE HOUSE
AND A GARDEN
AT
EDGWARE

COSTS FROM £900 TO £1,600

Or you can buy the land and build a house to your own design. A Building Plot will cost from £7 10s. to £10 per foot.

Edgware is situated 200 feet above ordnance datum. Main water-supply. Electricity: 7d. per unit for Lighting, 2¼d. per unit for power. Gas: 10·4d. per therm. Rates: 8s. 5d. in the £.
AND A TRAIN TO TOWN EVERY 8 MINUTES

Cheap Return Tickets are issued to Edgware on Saturdays and Sundays from most Underground Stations. Why not go there next week-end and stake your claim in Edgware Garden Suburb.

M2/10/26

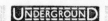

At Golders Green there was still plenty of land for new houses. 'Many house hunters who have not yet visited Golders Green will often have heard its name mentioned in connection with the garden city that has risen there.'

On the Empire Construction Company's Broadfields estate at Edgware, would-be purchasers were told that the homes were built on a site that was extremely high and that there were charming views. The developer promised that no inferior houses would spoil the area and that each house had a generous plot of land, so as to avoid overcrowding.

But no suburban district was considered mature until it had a cinema. In August 1931 work began on the Ritz Cinema at Edgware, and crowds of people watched the cranes erecting the steel framework and the bricklayers feverishly constructing the walls. By the 2nd May 1932 the building was ready for a gala opening: '*a worthy contribution to Edgware*', said the local newspaper.

Edgware station forecourt was also provided with shops and nearby was a large neo-Tudor public house with elaborate plasterwork that was somewhat reminiscent of Liberty's department store in Regent Street.

Soon multiple shops spread along the parades: F W Woolworth, J S Sainsbury, Montague Burton, together with smaller shops of every description. Edgware was virtually complete by the mid-1930s, and Frank Pick and Lord Ashfield were already thinking of those virgin green fields of Hertfordshire, just to the north of Edgware terminus. The Northern line to Elstree featured in addition to their 1935–40 New Works Plan, but it was a dream that was never to be fulfilled.

Crowds in a holiday mood at Colindale Station for the Annual RAF Air Display at nearby Hendon Aerodrome. The shows began in July 1920 (although Hendon had long been famous for air displays) and lasted until the late 1930s, when aircraft became too fast and too large for safe displays. Colindale Station was badly damaged by bombs in the Second World War.

EDGWARE

Live in an Old World Village
of Pleasant Surroundings

WITH

THROUGH TRAINS

TO AND FROM

The CITY & WEST END

UNDERGROUND

The Surrey Suburbs.

The extension of the City & South London tube to Morden was the only Underground line to penetrate into the Surrey suburbs in the 20th century. The network of lines inherited by the old Southern Railway had virtually created a monopoly of rail transport, except in the built-up old suburbs where trams were important. Indeed, with the formation of the Southern Railway in 1923 and Sir Herbert Walker's impressive plans for electrification, one finds it hard to justify the construction of any tube line south of Clapham or the Elephant & Castle, unless for a short section, to capture traffic from the trams and buses of the inner suburbs.

But the Underground group thought that there was ample scope. The Underground system was also attractive to many south Londoners, who admired the safe, swift Underground of north London – smart and bright stations, and trains so frequent that one didn't need a timetable; trains that took you direct to the office or Oxford Street stores without a change; a system where the signs were easy to understand.

The City & South London Railway – the pioneer tube line – was being modernised, and its narrow bore tunnels were converted to standard diameter at this time. A link was also constructed with the Hampstead tube at Charing Cross, so that eventually trains could run from either Highgate or Edgware southwards towards Morden via either the West End or the City. The section from Euston to Moorgate was closed from the 9th August 1922 until the 20th April 1924 for this work to be carried out. A further section was closed from Moorgate to Clapham Common from the 29th November 1923 to the 1st December 1924.

The plans for the southward extension to what was to be called 'North Morden' and a link from there with a proposed Wimbledon and Sutton railway were discussed in the early 1920s. But even Frank Pick and Lord Ashfield were no match for John Elliot of the Southern Railway. He was just as fanatical a publicist as they were, and the Southern Electric slogans and ever-expanding electrification schemes were impressive. He thought that the proposed extension of the tube was a 'brutal intrusion into the area'. Nevertheless, a deal with the Southern was struck.

As part of the deal, the Wimbledon & Sutton powers went to the Southern Railway, and it was built by them, but was not a success, as the Underground secured almost all the traffic over the area south of Morden by arranging feeder bus services with through road/tube tickets. However, even as late as 1944, there was talk at London Transport's headquarters at 55 Broadway of eventually reaching North Cheam.

Work began on the City & South London extension to Morden (the 'North' by then having been dropped) on the 31st December 1923. The line was in tube tunnels to just north of Morden terminus, the area thus far having become largely built up by 1914. The line then continued south to the car sheds.

There were difficulties at Tooting Broadway where a subterranean reservoir was encountered. The severe winter of 1924-25 also delayed the works – particularly the clearing of the ground and the building of the car sheds at Morden.

During the latter part of 1925 and the beginning of 1926, the rolling stock was being delivered from the manufacturers and had to be taken by road along narrow lanes to the depot.

The stations along the line were designed by Adams, Holden & Pearson and were specially built to stand out amid the 19th century streets and shopping centres. They were best seen at night, where their floodlit facades were like beacons in the gloom of the south London suburbs – guiding lights that shone the way to the fast and clean trains that took you to the bright lights of the West End, or home to toast and tea beside the open fire of one of the new houses that spread all too quickly over the north Surrey fields.

The Morden extension was opened by Lieut-Colonel J T C Moore-Brabazon MP, the Parliamentary Secretary to the Minister of Transport. He drove the special train from Clapham South to Morden. There was the usual official lunch – held in the car sheds, where the tables were decorated with red and white carnations. Speakers at the lunch expressed high hopes for the line's future and possibly its extension. But Lord Ashfield emphasised that any further tube extensions would have to create sufficient traffic to pay their way.

CLAPHAM COMMON —— MORDEN.
CITY & SOUTH LONDON RAILWAY.

COMMENCING THE
NEW EXTENSION LINE.

WATERLOW & SONS, LTP LONDON, DUNSTABLE & WATFORD.

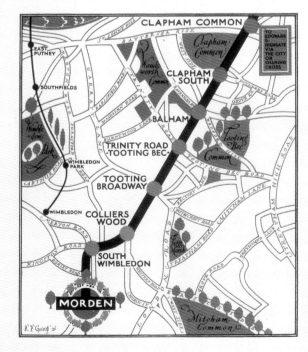

The Underground
presents its Compliments to
The South West Suburbs
and offers them its Services
for quick and easy Travel
to all parts of London

R.S.V.P.
at the Booking Offices   September 1926

Morden terminus, very like Edgware in its design at track level, had a small canopy over what was to be the pavement providing a bus station for the many routes that would connect districts such as Wallington, Cheam, Worcester Park, Mitcham, Banstead, Sutton and Esher. At first, though, Morden stood alone in the flat fields, except for a couple of rows of old cottages and the 'Crown Inn'. On the 31st July 1927, a large garage opened opposite the station, owned by an Underground subsidiary, Morden Station Garage Limited. Here one could park the car or bicycle for the day and travel up to London on the tube. The place was soon full and, by the end of that year, half a million people were using the trains each week at Morden alone. Overcrowding began to make life difficult for those living nearer London.

By the time the London County Council's St Helier estate was well under construction, the Morden line had become a byword for overcrowding. St Helier was laid out on 825 acres of farm land south of Morden and was completed in 1934. The estate had its own shops, and there were connecting bus routes to Morden, where long shopping parades soon grew along the country roads, to be joined by public houses and the inevitable cinema.

By the mid-1930s, travel on the Morden line was becoming a daily horror for thousands. Matters came to a head in 1937, when passengers staged a series of sit-in strikes when they heard that their train was to be 'turned short' of its advertised destination. The Morden line overcrowding became an issue in Parliament.

The Minister of Transport, E Leslie Burgin, urged London business firms to stagger their working hours. But little was done.

Sir Herbert Walker was not very pleased when he saw a drop in passenger traffic at Southern Railway's north Surrey stations. In spite of all the discomfort about which they bitterly complained, people still wanted the tube because it took them right into the centre of London instead of a vast and draughty terminus from which they still had to travel to the centre. At weekends, when the working week was over, the tube could also take them to the new suburbs of north London. 'From the hills of Middlesex to the hills of Surrey' was a publicity slogan at the time.

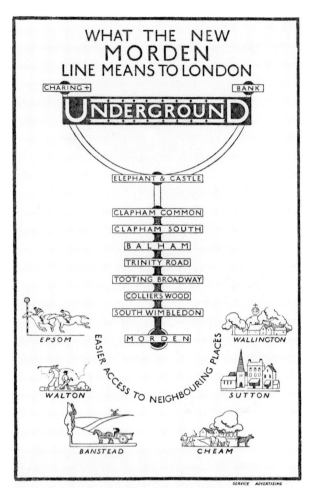

Facing page top **The station and the old village at Morden. 'Morden was just all green hedges . . . I watched Morden being built . . . that's when everything started to change: it was no longer in the depths of the country,' recorded a local resident. In the distance in this photograph are the trees of Morden Park and Morden Hall (built 1750). It was the home of the Hatfeild family, snuff manufacturers. Gilliat Hatfeild, the last owner, died in 1941.**

Facing page bottom **Morden station in June, 1927, with the shops built, and about to open for trade. A 165 Bus waits to run to Banstead, but there are still more cycles than cars.**

There were proposals for a relief tube line to be built from Kennington to Morden and Epsom, and one forward-looking estate developer in North Cheam advertised on a large board at the entrance to his estate: '*Coming this way . . .*' accompanied by a picture of a tube train.

But rising costs of materials in the late 1930s, coupled with doubts that in the end the line would not pay its way, resulted in abandonment of the plans. The London and Home Counties Traffic Advisory Committee and a group of seven north Surrey councils urged more trains. But with the line's signalling system and the 'standard' type of rolling stock, with its space-wasting motor cars, little could be done.

In 1938 the London Passenger Transport Board's Chief Mechanical Engineer, W S Graff-Baker, introduced the first of a large number of new tube trains, where the traction motors were placed beneath the floors, so increasing the passenger space. More cars of this type were manufactured than almost any other design of train in the world! (The very last 1938 stock trains ran on the Northern line as late as 1988). For a time at least, the overcrowding became less of a problem.

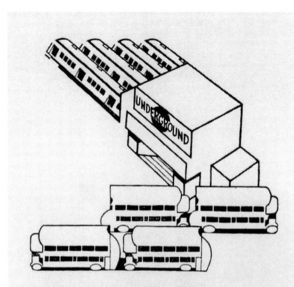

MR. BROWN'S HALF-WAY HOUSE

Mr. Brown lives at Rosehill, and travels by bus each morning to the Underground Station at Morden—the Half-Way House between his country seat and London Town. Morden Station is also the Half-Way House for Mr. Green of Nonsuch; Mr. White of Angel Bridge; Mr. Black of Cheam Common; Mr. Gray of Carshalton; and Mr. Rose of Stonecot Hill. There are separate bus routes for each, and from Morden Station a choice of trains to the City and West End; a choice renewed every five minutes and, whatever the choice, the journey takes just over thirty minutes, and no more.

Six wives, too, have discovered that a country life is the thing when they can visit the West End shops and theatres just as often and conveniently as when they lived in Town.

There are dozens of Browns, Greens, Whites, Blacks, Grays, and Roses living in the districts named. You need not envy them. You may join them. There is plenty of room for you, and the more who travel the better the bus and railway services will become.

Late 1920s poster advertising the convenience of suburban living in the districts around Morden station with its excellent bus connections.

New rolling stock was introduced from 1938 for the busy Northern Line. The 1938 stock was the first to have the traction motors under the floor, thus freeing space for more seats.

It's 7.16 am and a mixed crowd of blue and white collar workers rush to board a train for London one day in 1927. So popular was the new line that the trains were full to the doors by the time they reached Tooting.

Morden station and surrounding roads in the early 1930s. The railway tracks pass under the road to the depot, although the large building alongside – seen here at the bottom of the picture – was a garage, where in those days, passengers could leave their cycles or cars.

3
BUILDING A
NEW AGE

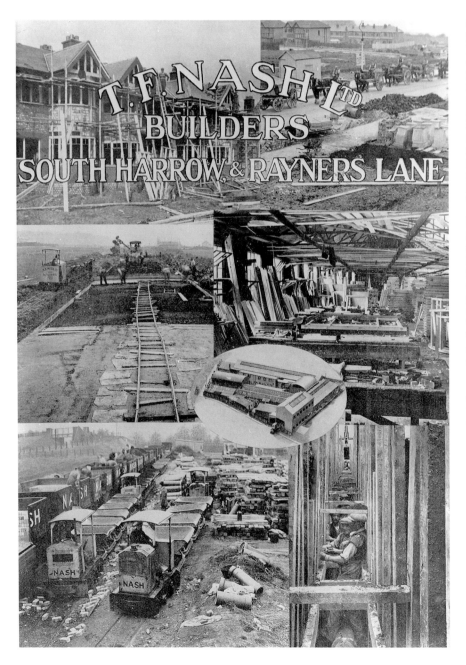

Cover of a T F Nash brochure, 1933. Their South Harrow developments eventually linked up with their estate at Rayners Lane. The picture at the bottom left-hand corner of the brochure shows the narrow-gauge railway system used for transporting goods from a special siding at Rayners Lane on what is now High Worple.

Facing page top **A view of the Rayners Lane station building in September 1929, as the first steps towards the construction of the new suburb are taken. The elm-lined meadows towards North Harrow would soon become part of Harrow Garden Village and Imperial Drive.**

Facing page bottom Alexandra Avenue, crossing the old sewerage farm and shooting ranges of Newton Farm in 1933. Rayners Lane station is on the horizon. On the left by the junction with Eastcote Lane is a hayrick at the yard of old Tithe Farm. One of the last tenant farmers here was Alfred Priest who died in 1916. The Tithe Farm Hotel was later built on the site. In December 1935 Nash advertised flats along Alexandra Avenue to rent at 23/6d to 24/11d per week.

Uxbridge Line Developments.

Along the Harrow and Uxbridge branch, the post-First World War years were quiet at first. But with the sale of various country estates (notably Swakeleys at Ickenham and Hillingdon Court at Hillingdon), developments began at Ickenham and North Hillingdon from about 1922 onwards, also in the Ruislip village area. At Long Lane, Ickenham, an additional station was opened and named Hillingdon in 1923.

The Swakeleys estate was then being laid out in plots for high-class housing by Stedman & Clarke and, at about the same time, the Cowley builder, Try, was starting to erect exclusive houses in generous wooded plots in the Sweetcroft Lane/Blossom Way area of Hillingdon.

But it was at the then lonely spot of Rayners Lane, where the Metropolitan had a junction with the District Railway (so bleak in winter that the windswept platforms were known as Pneumonia Junction), that the first large-scale housing development took place. This was the Metropolitan's Harrow Garden Village estate, which was begun in August 1929. The builder was E S Reid, who paid for his own sidings so that building materials could be delivered direct. The projected layout of the Garden Village was never completed. Other developers eventually moved in, but the Reid houses remained an attractive development amid oak and elm trees long after Rayners Lane ceased to be rural. One brochure persuaded Londoners to visit Harrow Garden Village, assuring them that 'on all sides of the estates were green fields and rural lanes. The air is clear and refreshing and there are upwards of 16 acres reserved for open space, tennis courts and recreation gardens'.

South of the station, the vast estate built by T F Nash of Harrow was started in about 1931. By 1934 the firm described itself as: 'the Builder of the Future . . . over 4,000 houses constructed in the Harrow and Ruislip areas, providing homes for 14,000 people. Over 1,000 men employed.' Nash had its own joinery works at Wealdstone. The basic design was for blocks of four or six terraced houses, with mock Tudor facings, although later types had cream walls and imitation window shutters (normally in dark green) or curved 'suntrap' windows in the art deco style.

American-style publicity announces the Rayners Lane estate of T F Nash, the prolific Harrow builder. The huge archway (in white, red and green) was erected by the junction of the new Warden Avenue and Alexandra Avenue in July 1934. The line of white posts marks the forecourt of the first parade of Nash shops. The cars are almost certainly part of Nash's courtesy fleet, but give the impression that the road has already been completed. In fact, the alignment of old Rayners Lane with the station ticket office can be seen through the arch.

'One word describes the Nash Estate – satisfaction,' ran the publicity, and the London evening newspapers carried advertisements with the headline: *'From Piccadilly to the 'Pic' of the houses'*, with an illustration of one of the Piccadilly line experimental streamlined trains. Another advertisement for the Nash houses claimed that living at Rayners Lane would be all peace and quiet, a place 'where the din and turmoil of the streets are exchanged for an aspect of spreading landscapes . . . of trees and green pastures where the only sounds are of birds.'

But it was all fantasy, for within weeks of taking up residence in your neat terraced house, with its black and white tiled bathroom and power points in every room, the next road had been completed, and the footings for another road after that and so on, right the way south towards Eastcote Lane, or west to where old Field End Road came down from Eastcote. Nowhere was as built up as this vast estate, although the years have seen the trees, which were carefully planted in the narrow avenues, mature and provide some greenery. The only open land was a few acres reserved for allotments.

But with a home of your own for £595, and a vast array of shops along Alexandra Avenue leading to Rayners Lane station, people were content. No aspect of publicity was overlooked in order to sell the estate. In about 1934 a grand shopping week was held and a temporary arch was built over Alexandra Avenue. Bedecked with flags, there was a bold sign proclaiming 'Nash Houses . . . the summit of High Value'. Cheap evening tickets were available on the Metropolitan and Piccadilly lines for prospective purchasers, and elaborate firework displays at Rayners Lane became commonplace. E S Reid also held a similar series of bonfire and firework nights on the Pinner side of the line to advertise the Harrow Garden Village estate.

Growth was rapid: in 1930 Rayners Lane was handling 22,000 passengers a year; by 1937 the total was a staggering 4,000,000! London Transport had to provide a temporary covered booking office and accommodation until the striking new station building was opened in 1938. Its bulky tower with long windows and flanking wings was by R H Uren in the Holden family style. The booking hall was built out over the side pavements, with ever-open sets of doors so that one could freely pass through the building. The station was sited at the highest point in the area and could be likened to a local beacon, either beckoning people to their daily labours in London or tempting them to the delights of shopping and shows in the West End.

Rayners Lane did not finally blend into Eastcote until 1940, although the development of the area around Eastcote station had begun as early as about 1912. However, it was W A Telling who began the modern development with houses in Morford Way soon after the First World War.

Parades of shops gradually replaced meadows and old cottages, and the last of the famous poplar trees along Field End Road were felled. The Pavilion Tea Gardens were sold for development in 1935, and Laings began their large estate. The show houses could be inspected after dark in the autumn by means of the then unique idea of floodlighting the roads.

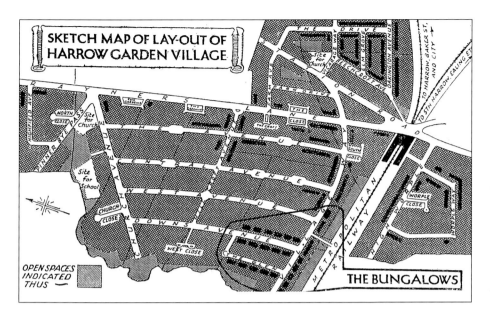

SKETCH MAP OF LAY-OUT OF HARROW GARDEN VILLAGE.

OPEN SPACES INDICATED THUS

THE BUNGALOWS

Rayners Lane station (opened 1906) was named after John Rayner, whose small farmhouse was along the muddy lane near Pinner. When development began in 1929, Harrow Garden Village was chosen as the name for the area especially north of the railway. For many years afterwards (and even as late as the 1950s) the local residents wanted the suffix "For Harrow Garden Village" after Rayners Lane on the station signs.

Ruislip Manor was one of the largest private housing estates. The developer was Manor Homes, associated with T F Nash. This is the start of the estate as seen from Ruislip Manor halt in May 1933. The white concrete ribbon of what would become Victoria Road can be seen in the background. To the older residents of Ruislip village, this estate 'was the beginning of the end of rural Ruislip'.

Nash may have been in the forefront of modern building, but seems to have employed good old-fashioned horses and carts. A splendid line-up on one of the estate roads.

Nash held a grand bonfire and fireworks night at Rayners Lane in November 1931 to attract prospective buyers. This display at Ruislip Manor is in September 1933 and was launched by the music hall stars, Elsie and Doris Walters. By 1937 some 1,800 houses had been completed, and Ruislip Manor station was handling a million passengers a year.

T F Nash was busy with superior-type houses east of Field End Road towards Eastcote village, and Comben & Wakeling's large neo-Tudor houses were in an attractive setting on the Eastcote Park estate, overlooking green meadows beside the river Pinn.

'Safeguard your dependants . . . it costs no more,' recommended the advertisements for the £1,075 houses on the Towers estate by Howell & Burgess, off Bridle Road. Rotherham Estates and the General Housing Company were other Eastcote builders of that period. But the final completion of the shops and the estates begun before the war had to wait until the 1950s.

Ruislip Manor halt had opened in 1912 in conjunction with the Ruislip Garden suburb scheme. There was no development south of the railway until 1933. Then work began on another vast estate which is said to have been the largest private development by any single building company at that time. Geo. M Ball (Manor Homes) were closely associated with T F Nash, and the design of the houses was similar. Because of the distance from the Metropolitan Railway sidings at Ruislip, a light railway system was laid down for the building supplies. Some of the working areas were nearly two miles to the south, near South Ruislip.

Soon acre after acre of the flat, elm-lined fields were replaced by roads, crescents and closes. The main artery was Victoria Road, which took the route of the boulevard planned in the Ruislip Garden City Plan of 1909. Parades of shops appeared south of the Ruislip Manor halt, and by 1936–37 the narrow under-bridge was widened.

'Even those who feel a preference for the delights of man-made civilisation invariably find that if their days are to be spent in the big city, they are happy to return, in the quiet dusk of the evenings, to nature's stronghold outside the town,' enthused the Manor Homes brochure. At Ruislip each house was a 'palace in miniature', and prices started at £450 for a two-bedroomed home, with weekly repayments of 12s 2d (61p) after payment of a £5 deposit.

'Travelling only half-an-hour from London, you will find an estate still retaining the unmarred beauties amid the unspoiled, healthy atmosphere of Nature in her most beautiful aspects.' Three-bedroomed terraced houses were £665, and there was a 'sun-trap' window house for £745. Stained

Eastcote, on the Metropolitan Uxbridge branch, opened on 26th May 1906, not long before this picture was taken. Its wooden platforms were later lengthened to accommodate the large crowds of visitors that came in summer to sample the tea gardens of the old village.

Eastcote's main shopping street. The old line of poplar trees – once a distinctive feature – were felled for parades of useful shops. Street lighting was provided from December 1925. Here are the Midland Bank, Boots Cash Chemists, Cato the ironmonger, Tru-Form and Bata for shoes. Across the road is the Manor House public house opened in July 1933 in a typical 'Tudorbethan' style. Next to it was Field End Hall, built by Tellings to serve their new housing development. In February 1931 it was converted into the Ideal Cinema. From 1st March of that year it showed sound films. It had fairly comfortable seats available from 8d to 2s 4d.

glass was fitted to all hall and landing windows. Each house had a kitchenette with Ideal hot water boiler (coke and coal bunkers were usually sited immediately outside the kitchen in the back garden), gas-heated copper for clothes washing, draining boards in best wood and a deep sink with chromium-plated taps.

Food could be kept hygienically in a well-ventilated larder, and there were kitchen cabinets and an electric ironing point. The happy housewife had the additional attraction of free light fittings throughout the house. A final touch of luxury for the 'man of small means' was a £975 house with four bedrooms. Ruislip-Northwood Council feared, however, that so many relatively cheap houses would not produce the high rates they could have got from an estate of larger properties.

In October 1933, Piccadilly line trains began to run through to Uxbridge and, with the increased transport facilities, the houses began to sell quickly. Manor Homes thereupon provided the amenity of a public hall. This was followed by the erection of St Paul's Church, consecrated in November 1936.

In 1934 a monthly season ticket on the Piccadilly line from Ruislip to Green Park cost £1 13s 0d (£1.65), or by Metropolitan Railway to Baker Street £1 14s 0d (£1.70). The old village street had already been transformed during the 1920s into a modern shopping centre. The real seal of civilisation came in 1929, when, on the 3rd September, crowds came to the official opening of the Rivoli Cinema. A free car park and a tea lounge were additional attractions to the 1,000 seater auditorium which was wired for 'talkie' films. Later Ruislip had a second cinema, the Astoria in High Street. South of Ruislip station, Shenley Avenue was being built by H Bowers: '. . . *the Ruislip Station Estate . . . the estate that's different. Lose no time in paying the estate a visit, for the dream house you have yearned for is waiting to be secured at a price easily within your reach.*'

Bowers offered purchasers magnificent Aztec-style fireplaces, whilst the bathrooms had chromium-plated taps and coloured pedestal basins and baths. The fanlight windows on the landings and above the main glass of the bays were coloured. The rising sun motif was a popular feature in the design.

Visitors to the estate who made their way over the narrow railway bridge and down the still rural West End Road with white-painted wooden railings saw ancient Sherleys Farm on the left, and beyond a bend in the road they were welcomed by the estate's sales staff. It was Bowers' ploy to request would-be purchasers to call on one of the families already in residence on the estate to obtain their unsolicited opinion on the houses before making a final decision, so great was Bowers' confidence in their product!

Across West End Road, Taylor Woodrow began to fill in the fields towards the GWR main line with some roads of semi-detached bungalows. Each had two bedrooms, a well fitted kitchenette and a small dining room but, most attractive of all, a large lounge complete with a fireplace that incorporated a fitted wireless set. At Hill Farm estate, off Sharps Lane, buyers were told of the 'unusual and extensive views . . . of well wooded and undulating country-side'. For once, this was actually true.

Along the road to Eastcote village and north of Eastcote Road, the Metropolitan Railway Country Estates were building houses of a style very similar to those at Harrow Garden Village. Once again, the virtues of being close to the magnificent Ruislip Woods and the river Pinn were emphasised.

Ruislip High Street, as we have already mentioned, was becoming 'daily more like Ealing Broadway', to quote a local press article. The Poplars tea gardens, famous in early Metro-land days, lay derelict and overgrown until about 1935, to be replaced by a parade of shops that included some typical household names of the period: Salmons, the ironmongers, where the smell of paraffin, cornmeal and household cleaners gave a safe and old-fashioned atmosphere for the new suburban dwellers to savour; the ABC teashop, with its smell of fresh bread wafting across the end of Ickenham Road towards Boots Cash Chemists with apothecary jars in the window, and J S Sainsbury, where young men in high buttoned white jackets busied themselves slicing bacon at a machine, cutting cheese with a wire or patting fresh butter into shape for waiting customers. At the end of the shop, in classical splendour of polished mahogany and pillars, sat the cashier, who also took orders for goods to be delivered.

QUALITY *plus* ECONOMY

I F you are seeking a worth-while house—a house representing "rock-bottom" value plus true artistic merit, then you should lose no time in inspecting the really wonderful Bowers built houses that are now being sold as fast as they are built on the Ruislip Manor Garden Estate, Ruislip, Middlesex. They are being constructed with a generous disregard of the ordinary measures of cheapening production and many features, usually only to be found in much more expensive houses, are incorporated in their design.

There are a host of exclusive types from which to choose, rang ng from £945 to £1,175 freehold, and in addition to there being no road charges, legal costs or stamp fees to pay, there is available to all purchasers a remarkably convenient system of gradual payment that renders purchase no more costly than rent.

The houses can be inspected any day, including Sunday, and our representatives, who are always available, will readily answer any question or explain any point without obligating you in the slightest degree. Free booklet and travel voucher for the asking.

BOWERS, LTD.,

Ruislip Manor Garden Estate.

Telephone—Ruislip 217.

Bridge widening at Ruislip Manor began in January 1936.

Bowers built several estates in Ruislip. Their Station estate along West End Road/Shenley Avenue was described in glowing terms: 'Lose no time in paying the estate a visit, for the dream house you have yearned for is waiting . . . at a price easily within your reach'. It was in one of their bungalows in 1960 that the Russian spies the Krugers operated!

Ruislip High Street in 1930, with St Martin's Church and the old village centre. Development here was piecemeal. The shops seen here date from the 1920s, whilst the southern section of High Street (originally part of West End Road) was not finally completed until later. Fabbs Restaurant on the right was famous for its dinner-dances. In May 1938 Inwards Garage took over the site and opened a palatial car showroom and garage.

High Street, Ruislip.

Hillingdon station was opened on the 10th December 1923. After requests by local residents, the name was changed to Hillingdon (Swakeleys) in April 1924. The old station closed in 1992, being replaced by a re-sited and very state of the art structure in conjunction with the new A40 underpass – so different from this photograph which was taken near the site of the present Western Avenue and Master Brewer Hotel. Various estate developers' huts can just be seen on the bridge. The road was widened in 1938.

The Scotch Wool & Hosiery Stores farther down Ruislip High Street, near the new F W Woolworth store, was well stocked with wool for housewives to start their winter evening knitting. Woolworths had replaced the barns and cows of Wilkins Farm. On the opposite side of High Street was Lyttons' department store, which included a restaurant with potted palms, Lloyd-loom chairs and glass-topped tables.

Down near the remaining buildings of the old Ruislip (protected by a local society), there was Williams Bros, the north London grocers. When the shop opened in 1936, eggs were offered at 1s 3d (6p) per dozen. Thrifty shoppers quickly patronised the store, for after spending a small amount they received a thin metal token with their change. Once or twice a year, they could take back the tokens and receive a cash refund for their value. A similar scheme was operated by another suburban grocery chain in the Underground suburbs – Payantake.

Despite the press announcement in 1936 that Ruislip had ceased to be a holiday resort, the opening of the Lido at Ruislip Reservoir just to the north of the town on the 20th May was a grand occasion. Music, as well as 100 shapely ladies from the League of Health & Beauty, plus a cabaret in the art deco pavilion building put Ruislip Lido on the map for water sports and as a substitute beach for children during their school holidays.

Ickenham developed slowly, although some of the larger plots on the Swakeleys estate were eventually sub-divided, and smaller houses were built by R T Warren. Along Ickenham High Road,

work started on the Drummond estate in 1923. The builders announced that the oak trees would be preserved, as Queen Elizabeth had once picnicked beneath them! But local residents were more concerned about unmade-up roads and bad drains in the village. Much road widening was also required. Old Back Lane, leading to Uxbridge, was transformed in 1937 into a dual carriageway named Swakeleys Road. The old elm-lined and muddy road from Ruislip to Hillingdon was also improved out of all recognition. There was also much tree-planting with some magnificent flowering varieties.

The Ivy House estate, with its 'unbeatable suntrap bungalows' at Hoylake Crescent offered the young housewife of 1936 a 12ft x 10ft kitchen with 'every modern device . . . a real treasure'. Advertisements in the London papers asked: 'Getting married? See the splendid suntrap houses and bungalows at Ickenham.'

The Ickenham Hall estate at Milton Court on the site of Milton Farm was only partly finished before the start of the Second World War in 1939. The builders, Brown & Langford, had a large theatrical-style board with three-dimensional figures announcing the estate in Swakeleys Road: 'Magnificent Milton Court . . . procure while you may.'

Hillingdon village proper was over a mile from the Underground station, which was actually on the Ickenham side of the new Western Avenue (A40). The shopping parades at North Hillingdon grew after the Western Avenue was opened here in 1936. A Metropolitan Railway brochure of some years before said of the new Hillingdon: 'The estate is rising on ground which till recently belonged to parkland of Hillingdon Court. The country adjoining Hillingdon Station has no superior in the neighbourhood for quiet beauty, and the popularity of the new suburb is already well assured.'

Hillingdon Mount estate was 'carried out on unusual lines, affording amenities to residents not generally met with, and a large area has been reserved for tennis courts.' A house and garage on this Metropolitan Railway estate could be bought for a down-payment of £5 and £800 mortgage. The Hillingdon Estates Company had houses for £725 upwards: '. . . *filled with all those conveniences so dear to the heart of the housewife. The roads are wide and there is space to ensure that purchasers have plenty of fresh air and good gardens.*'

The developers of the Tudor Way estate off Long Lane offered people a free lift by car from Hillingdon station. The new shopping centre under construction would be pointed out as they sped along. '*A model Tudor Village of charming houses artistically grouped in the form of green courtyards,*' prospective purchasers read in the brochure. There was even an impressive Tudor-style gateway, which still exists, at the entrance to the estate.

With the arrival of the Western Avenue and improved transport facilities, including buses to Hayes and Uxbridge, Ickenham and Ruislip, cheaper houses were being built, and eventually prices for these were as low as £345. 'Britain's Wonder Houses,' read a hoarding opposite Hillingdon station. But much countryside still remained and, even today, there are green fields between Ickenham and South Ruislip – as well as Northolt Airport.

Uxbridge has remained more of a London country town than an Underground suburb, and there was really little large-scale building in the period between the two World Wars. The clanging trams were replaced by silent trolleybuses in 1936. The old Belmont Road station, which had waited in vain for any possible extension of the Metropolitan line into Buckinghamshire, was closed and replaced by a new three-track terminus in High Street in December 1938. The architect was L H Bucknell. The interior of the station bears a close resemblance to that of Cockfosters. There are stained-glass windows representing local heraldic devices, designed by Ervin Bossanyi.

Thoroughly Modern.

During the 1930s builders offered all kinds of inducements to buy. It was bewildering and very exciting. There were free tickets to visit new estates by Underground, and most house builders offered interior decoration to choice. Some of the more expensive houses had 'fitted kitchens'. Black and white dado tiles broke up the sanitary white of the new bathrooms. The great London stores offered a wide array of furniture. The range of house designs was wide and within financial reach of most young marrieds struggling to keep their heads above water during the depressions of the early 1930s.

Osbert Lancaster lampooned the London suburbs of the day with a series of cartoons depicting styles such as 'Modernistic', 'By-pass Variegated' and 'Wimbledon Transitional'. It was the age of Art Deco – in these homes *radios lurked in tea caddies and bronze nudes burst asunder at the waistline to reveal cigarette lighters. Nothing is what it seems'*. The novelist J B Priestley saw how people went to look over 'these new houses, seeing them as a kind of signpost pointing to a sunlit main road of life'.

Although the economic depression had hit London hard, things improved quicker in London and south-eastern England than elsewhere. By 1936 unemployment in Middlesex, with its gleaming new factories along the Great West Road, was down to 4.5 per cent, as compared with 33.4 per cent in Glamorgan, for example. The new factories attracted people from far and wide and, once they had a regular job, they could look around for a house with only £25 in their pockets.

Inside the new home, London furnishers had immediate solutions. Waring & Gillow offered bedroom suites for £10 10s, complete with triple mirrored dressing table.

For the kitchen, Catesby of Tottenham Court Road offered a kitchen cabinet with glass doors for under £5, the cabinet being filled with free packets of Hudson's Soap Powder, Lux Flakes and the new Oxydol. There was also a packet of cocoa for a nightcap! Most builders offered free gas coppers for the weekly wash. Refrigerators were so rare that anyone claiming to have one would be besieged by neighbours seeking to keep some perishable luxury in safety!

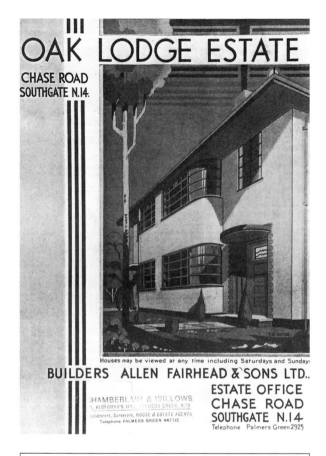

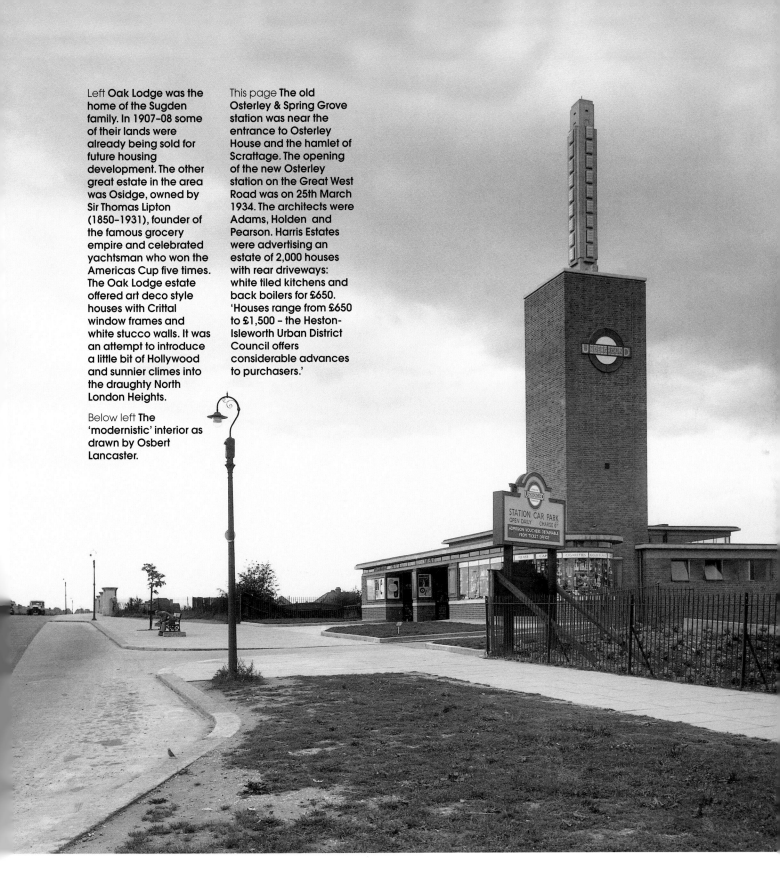

Left **Oak Lodge was the home of the Sugden family. In 1907–08 some of their lands were already being sold for future housing development. The other great estate in the area was Osidge, owned by Sir Thomas Lipton (1850–1931), founder of the famous grocery empire and celebrated yachtsman who won the Americas Cup five times. The Oak Lodge estate offered art deco style houses with Crittal window frames and white stucco walls. It was an attempt to introduce a little bit of Hollywood and sunnier climes into the draughty North London Heights.**

Below left **The 'modernistic' interior as drawn by Osbert Lancaster.**

This page **The old Osterley & Spring Grove station was near the entrance to Osterley House and the hamlet of Scrattage. The opening of the new Osterley station on the Great West Road was on 25th March 1934. The architects were Adams, Holden and Pearson. Harris Estates were advertising an estate of 2,000 houses with rear driveways: white tiled kitchens and back boilers for £650. 'Houses range from £650 to £1,500 – the Heston-Isleworth Urban District Council offers considerable advances to purchasers.'**

Temples of Escapism.

The 1930s were years of innovation and rapid change. Fashion designs were fluid. It was the age of sun and cloud and streaming hair motifs. Some have tried to equate the rising sun and the youthful figures of Art Deco design with the spirit of Jugendherben, particularly after 1933, with the rise of the Nazi party in Germany. It was an age when it was good to be young and not to look forward to the future, even though things appeared to be better than just after 1918. It was a good time to try to enjoy life.

The cinema, with the advent of the 'talkie' age, became the most important building in London's suburbs. 'The cinema fills a need in our lives which no preceding age has ever felt,' confided F Morton Shand in 1930 before the real explosion of the cinema took place. C Day Lewis's remark about 'cinemas before churches' reflected the feeling – simple wooden huts often served as new parish churches for the growing housing estates around London.

Cinemas, in fact, became the social centres of the time. With seats for matinees as low as 4d (less than 2p) if you queued early, everyone could afford escapism in those days which were still lacking television. Housewives, most of whom left the workforce on marriage, slipped away for a quiet cry at Hollywood love dramas in the enveloping darkness of the cinema on weekday afternoons, whilst on Saturdays there would be family outings to watch the mighty Wurlitzer organ rise from the cinema pit during the interval when Eldorado ice-cream would be on sale. There was also live entertainment on the cinema stage on occasions: and, when it was all over, there were the cheerful red buses or Underground trains to whisk the family back home.

Soon, every London suburb, however new, had its Granada, Ritz or Odeon Cinema. The name Odeon has no classical association – it stood for Oscar Deutsch entertains our Nation! Thirty-four new sites opened in 1936 alone. Deutsch, the company head, kept Harry Weedon, his leading architect, busy designing medium-sized buildings which dwarfed their surroundings. They were the beacons of the bright new age, leaving behind for ever the dowdy streets of the past.

No successful suburb was without its cinema. This is the Odeon in Northolt Road, South Harrow. Designed by a Harrow architect A.P. Starkey, it opened in 1933 and it set the style for the many Odeon cinemas that opened all over the country. Long demolished, a block of flats stands on the site. Notice the gas lamp, contrasting with the Art Deco lines of the new building.

Inviting Doorways.

If the cinemas were temples of entertainment, the Underground stations were the temples of travel. Frank Pick, Vice-Chairman of the Underground Group, had called his stations 'inviting doorways in an architectural setting that cannot be missed by the casual passer-by'.

To live near an Underground station was considered by many people to be the 'acme of convenience'. The newer station buildings were designed to be wide and welcoming; the trains so frequent that you didn't need a timetable; the fares cheap enough for all. There were the well-lit colourful Underground trains and the platforms with their artistic posters, that provided a never-ending source of delight as they poured out from 55 Broadway year after year. No wonder people would walk miles to reach the Underground. Frank Pick and Charles Holden, his architect, had taken a trip round northern Europe in 1931 and, partly in consequence of this, the use of concrete, bronze and large windows became familiar features of Underground architecture.

Pick commissioned Edward Johnston to design a special type-face in 1916, to be used on Underground signs and publicity, and his attention to every detail of design and function became legendary. The Underground was seen as the safe, swift way around London during the 1930s. It was the gateway to the pleasures of the West End. 'To Town Tonight' was a publicity theme of Underground advertising for many years. London's hundreds of cinemas, theatres, concert halls, sports events, to say nothing of the cafes, restaurants and department stores, the exhibitions, circuses and pageantry, offered a seemingly endless variety of entertainment.

But after about 1937 there appears to have been a slackening off in evening travel to London. Homes were becoming more comfortable. The suburbs were beginning to mature and offered alternative social facilities: social clubs for the neighbourhood; tennis clubs; vast public houses which were sometimes neo-Georgian but more usually half-timbered; golf links. The wireless became universal: there was Children's Hour for junior family members; Radio Luxembourg and Radio Normandy for young adults.

The new station at Rayners Lane just after completion in 1938. The tall booking halls with generous glazing provided both a pleasant start or end to a journey and, on elevated sites like this one, a landmark advertising the presence of the Underground from a distance. Imperial Drive had been completed the previous year, linking Rayners Lane with Station Road at North Harrow. Cutlers and their associate Garnett & Co were the builders of much of North Harrow, and their estates linked up with Rayners Lane – also with developments by H Pickrill and others. The Cutler houses had stained glass windows in their halls and on their landings – made by the famous Whitefriars glass works at Wealdstone.

Lost Names and New Names.

Railways have frequently named their stations for traffic reasons instead of using long-standing place names that suffered from not being widely known. Well-known place names thereby swallowed up the names of neighbouring areas by the addition of compass point prefixes or suffixes. In the Harrow area, Hooking Green became North Harrow, Roxeth became South Harrow and Roxborough became West Harrow. What is now central Harrow was originally called Greenhill, with Harrow town upon its hill to the south.

The Piccadilly tube built the present Oakwood station midway between Barnet and Enfield, two miles west of the former and just under two miles east of the latter. Yet it originally decided to call the station East Barnet, changing this to Enfield West shortly before opening. Oakwood Park was half a mile to the south of the station and there was much local campaigning for this name, or plain Oakwood, to be used. This was in due course to be successful: Oakwood was added as a suffix in 1934, just over a year after the station opened, and the name became plain Oakwood in 1946.

Requests have on a number of occasions been made to have the name South Wimbledon (Northern line) changed to the correct name for the area, Merton, but to no avail – despite the fact that 'Merton Grove' was a name considered before opening. The district of Ickenham is blessed with three Underground stations, one named Ickenham, one named West Ruislip and one named Hillingdon. The junction of the A40 and B466 just south of Hillingdon station is now called Hillingdon Circus. Hillingdon itself is just over a mile to the south. Local residents successfully campaigned to have the suffix 'Swakeleys' added to Hillingdon station signs in 1934.

In other cases, stations were built on sites that had no obvious existing place name to use. Two stations that opened in 1933/4 received names that had been submitted in separate local press competitions: Queensbury – a play on the neighbouring Kingsbury – and Northwood Hills. Ten years earlier Northwick Park station had opened on the Metropolitan Railway. Instead of following the railway habit and calling it East Harrow or Kenton West, the name used came from the Northwick family who were the local Lords of the Manor. Northwick Park was the name of their country estate near Moreton-in-Marsh, Gloucestershire.

North of Finchley is West Finchley station and adjacent to Fortis Green is East Finchley station. Conversely, the old name of Woodside Park has survived further up the Northern line for the station next to the district generally known as North Finchley since the days of trams describing it as such. The names on this section of the Northern line pre-date the Underground, being in use when the Northern line took the station over in the 1930s.

Land between Harrow and Kenton had belonged to the Churchill-Rushout family, who had been lords of the Manor of Harrow. Their country seat was at Northwick Park, near Moreton-in-Marsh in the Cotswolds. Some of the roads at Northwick were named after Gloucestershire villages.

THE NORTHWICK ESTATE
NORTHWICK PARK & KENTON

LONDON'S NEW SUBURB

9 miles from the Marble Arch.
14 minutes from Baker Street.
Served by three Electric Railways.
Over 100 Trains each way every day.

A UNIQUE SPECIMEN OF TOWN PLANNING

The Largest and best laid out Estate near London.

Delightful & Artistic Freehold Houses for Sale

Each a distinctive Ideal Home in every sense of the word.
Splendidly built, only the best material being used.
Perfect rural surroundings, Lovely views, Extraordinarily healthy.
Well constructed Roads. Main Drainage. Electric Light and Gas, and Colne Valley Water.

WOODCOCK HILL LANE.

Left **The District Railway station at Roxeth, for which the new name South Harrow was coined, on the branch later taken over by the Piccadilly line.**

Below **Queensbury station was opened on 16th December 1934, two years after the railway to Stanmore. The name came as the result of a newspaper competition offering a £5 prize, though coincidentally or otherwise Queensbury Road in Kingsbury pre-dated the opening of Queensbury station by eight years. This photograph was taken on 25th September 1933. On the extreme right a sign advertises the Laing estate and its development of 1,000 houses.**

4
SUBURBAN
METRO-LAND

The Metropolitan Railway was the pioneer of suburban development – dating from the 19th century. Its extension line of the late 19th century had encouraged developments at Harrow, Pinner and Northwood. But it was the building of the branch to Uxbridge in 1904 that set the stage for the vast Metro-land developments after 1919.

The area around Wembley Park was virtually undeveloped before the British Empire Exhibition of 1924. But after the mid-1920s, housing estates began to grow along the roads and up the slopes of Barn Hill and Chalk Hill to the north of the Metropolitan line. A Metropolitan brochure of 1927 described this area as *'one of the healthiest spots near London . . . numerous houses are already being built or in course of erection. Hundreds of houses are being built in the neighbourhood, including Barn Hill, Townsend Park and Forty Lane'.*

Wembley Park had attracted day trippers long before the Exhibition. It was originally the estate of the Page family. In 1793 the celebrated landscapist, Humphrey Repton, laid out the grounds. In the 19th century, the estate was the home of the Grey family, and in 1880 they sold the lands to the Metropolitan Railway whose new line already cut through the northern edge of the property.

Sir Edward Watkin, the Metropolitan Railway's Chairman, wanted the Park as a pleasure ground for London. H E Milner was commissioned to design lakes, waterfalls, tea pavilions and floral gardens, as well as sports facilities, including a very fine running track.

A new station, Wembley Park, opened on the 12th May 1894, when the grounds were also opened to the public. Watkin also wanted the Park to be the site of his grandiose scheme for a tower similar to, but higher than, Eiffel's structure in Paris. After a competition, work on the Tower began in June 1893, the architects being Heenan & Froude of Blackpool Tower fame. But only the first stage was ever completed due to the fact that the public were apathetic and money ran out. The lifts eventually broke down, and the abandoned structure became known as the Red Tower or Watkin's Folly. It was finally cleared away in 1908.

An 18-hole golf course was laid out near the site of the future Stadium and was popular with City men and Army Officers during the First World War. There was also another golf course up on Barn Hill.

Clay pigeon shooting was a popular sport at Forty Farm, the tower here being a familiar landmark for Metropolitan Railway passengers. The land was sold by the end of the 1920s and developed by Haymills Ltd, with houses specially designed by R T Welch, Cachemaille-Day and Lander of Lincoln's Inn. The Tudor-style houses were popular with film and stage people and BBC folk.

At nearby Preston hamlet were the grounds of the Uxendon Shooting Club, and in 1908 the site was chosen for the Olympic Games Shooting Contests. The Club, with the support of the twenty seven inhabitants of the area, petitioned the Metropolitan Railway Company in March 1908 for a halt to be built at Preston Lane bridge. The Metropolitan agreed to build a simple, two-platform halt on the Wembley side of the bridge, provided that the Club paid half the cost. The two 260ft long platforms were opened on the 21st May 1908, the first train to stop there being the 12.05 pm from Baker Street. Names suggested had been Uxendon and Preston Road. The bleak platforms had long boards reading: 'Stop here for Uxendon Shooting School Club'.

AERIAL VIEW OF WEMBLEY

Above **The British Empire Exhibition of 1924–25 at Wembley brought millions of visitors to this formerly rural corner of Middlesex. The large buildings to the right are the Palaces of Engineering and of Industry. Beyond can be seen Wembley Park Drive and early suburban development. The edge of the Stadium is to the far left of the picture.**

Left **Looking over Wembley Park from the south in 1920. At the lower edge is Wembley Hill station. To the north of the parklands is the Metropolitan Railway (Wembley Park station is hidden by trees). Barn Hill and Chalk Hill can be seen. The island of trees in the middle of the park mark the site of Watkin's folly and that of the Stadium. The streets at the bottom left of the picture are on the pre-1914 Wembley Hill estate.**

Left **Haymills** built many fine detached houses on the slopes of Barn Hill, which had a golf course on its summit for many years. Part of the hill remains as open space. Later Haymills withdrew from the site, and other builders completed the development.

Above **Blackbird Cross** estate at Kingsbury was developed by C W B Simmonds who advertised the development as being 'amongst charming rural scenery'. Old Chalk Hill House survived until 1963. Blackbird Farm survived until the 1950s.

Facing Page **The Metropolitan Railway reached Harrow-on-the-Hill in 1880. But with the construction of the Great Central Railway to**

Marylebone at the end of the century, and the Metropolitan to Uxbridge in 1904, the station was extensively rebuilt. This is a view from 1908.

On the opposite side of the line, beyond the bridge, was the Harrow Golf Course, its distinctive club house with verandah being another local feature. In 1928 the Club had 400 members. The area also had some tea rooms set in orchards. In 1926 Preston Road was still a wayside halt, where visitors alighted to see the Grove estate. Here they could contemplate whether to buy a house from £1,025 – £1,185 on '. . . *a self-contained estate in the best part of Preston . . . only eight minutes from the station . . . carefully planned and soundly constructed . . . of artistic merit and varied design, in an orchard setting of particular charm.'* Preston offered a palliative for ' . . . *the nerves of strained Town workers . . . a place where pure air blows in from the Chilterns'.*

By 1930 a number of builders were at work, including The Bateman Building Company, Marshall's Estates and Clifford Sabey. The halt was rebuilt as a station in 1931 with C W Clark's shops flanking the entrance on the Harrow side of the bridge.

By the early 1930s the houses on the Barn Hill estate were reaching up to the road between the station and Preston. At this time the whole area was busy with builders' lorries and carts (many builders were still using horse transport). Everywhere there were stacks of bricks, piles of sand, bags of cement, freshly sawn timber and much mud; the smell of new paint, of surplus wood being burnt to clear the sites; various huts for workmen, architects and site foremen; here and there boards proclaiming the merits of the various developments.

'On fine summer Saturdays, Preston is one of the brightest places near London. To the north there are wide spaces of attractive, open countryside.'

Later, much of the area of fields was to be buried under the rapid developments that followed the opening of the Stanmore branch.

The Harrow Golf Course gave way to masses of smaller houses by the late 1930s, whilst the north side of the line was developed with high-class houses on the Woodcock Dell and Woodcock Hill estates on the site of the old Woodcock Dell Farmhouse and its lands. *'The large sports ground of Messrs Selfridge directly adjoins the estate, adding much to preserve the attractive features of the open countryside'*, advocated the 1931 edition of Metro-land.

As late as 1930, the Metro-land guide books still described the area around Harrow Hill as a place for a day trip: '. . . *a fascinating countryside of rich pastures lies around, yet whilst encircled by rural surroundings of primitive simplicity the town is, by Metro, within 15 minutes of Baker Street'.*

Below **Station Road, Harrow, in 1934.**
The arrival of the Metropolitan Railway in 1880 had heralded a rapid expansion of building across the fields between the new station and the original Harrow and Wealdstone LNWR station (hence Station Road). The animated scene in this view is dominated by the Coliseum Theatre, opened in 1929 by the local MP, Sir Oswald Mosley. For much of its life, it was a cinema, but reverted to live entertainment and classical concerts around the time of the Second World War. It was demolished, despite much protest, in July 1959.

Above **College Road**, with an ST type bus in the late 1930s. The tower of the old Baptist Church went in more recent times and the new Church has been built behind.

Beyond Harrow.

The first district the train reached after Harrow-on-the-Hill was North Harrow. By 1914, the western end of Harrow had reached out along the Pinner Road, mainly by the efforts of local builder, Albert Cutler. He resumed operations in the 1920s, and advertised extensively. In fact, Cutler was the builder of North Harrow! Yet, ever mindful of the main reason why people went to live in suburbs – the fresh air and nearby countryside – his publicity informed would-be purchasers: '*Ideal homes in North Harrow . . . for pedestrians who delight in rambles, the region might be called an enchanted ground.*'

So successful was the advertising that North Harrow halt was soon proving inadequate for the new commuters, and the station was rebuilt in 1929, although the wooden waiting rooms on the platforms, situated up on the railway embankment, were still rather primitive in appearance. The long gardens of the Cutler houses gave ample scope for gardeners, and soon the district was a riot of summer roses – climbers and standards – and neat lawns. The shopping centre included branches of the principal banks; Cullens, the high-class grocers; United Dairies; a wireless shop, and a chemist where you could buy a roll of Ilford film and, with the aid of the family box camera, try a few snaps of the children playing in the attractive new garden with Spot the dog!

The Headstone Hotel was an impressive, if rather gloomy, Olde English style pub by the station. It had a large hall for dances and meetings; but to ensure that everyone knew their place there was a separate bar for workmen!

A 1930 picture of North Harrow bridge, looking towards Station Road and its junction with Pinner Road.

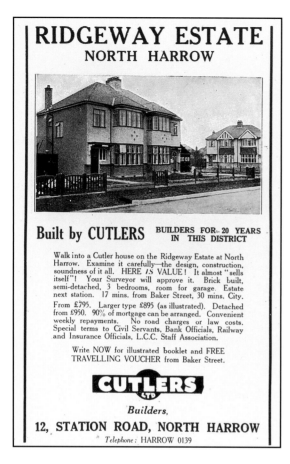

Cutlers and their associate Garnett & Co were the builders of much of North Harrow and their estates linked up with Rayners Lane – also with developments by H Pickrill and others. The Cutler houses had stained glass windows in their halls and on their landings – made by Whitefriars glass works at Wealdstone.

Cutler's houses eventually linked up with those of E S Reid and other builders at Rayners Lane, Imperial Drive being a fine new highway, opened in 1937, connecting the two places. In The Ridgeway, Cutler built his detached houses in four styles, with central heating and garages.

H Pickrill was another North Harrow builder, and with all this activity the 'Enchanted Ground' eventually all but disappeared. But there was some good tree-planting and even a tiny park. By the late 1930s blocks of elegant flats with green-tiled roofs appeared along the Pinner Road. The 'ultra-modern conveniences' included tennis courts, petrol pumps and garages, central heating, refrigerators and, in the main courtyard amid flower beds, an illuminated fountain.

Cannon Croft was the name of a house built off Eastcote Road in 1907 for the Rumens family. The General Housing Co built houses here in a variety of styles, including some detached properties with Art Deco windows. Their estate office was on the corner of Rosecroft Walk and Eastcote Road.

At Pinner the Metropolitan Railway's Surplus Lands' Grange Estate of 1920–1928, close to the station on the village side, had at least one house designed by C W Clark. Pinner's Cuckoo Hill estate, 'the City Man's Dream', was built by W Telling of Eastcote in 1928–1931. The detached houses were built along roads specially planted with flowering trees that over the years have made Pinner very much a green and wooded Underground suburb. The old village remained intact, except for Bridge Street. Here there was great activity in shop-building during the 1930s. The developers were very proud when they were able to tear down a picturesque Tudor farmhouse at the top of Bridge Street hill and replace it with the luxury Langham Cinema in just six months in 1935–1936.

But the most ambitious Metropolitan suburb along the 'Extension' line was between Pinner and Northwood. Here there were open fields until 1930, when two businessmen, H Peachey and Harry Neal, produced plans for a completely new suburb. A competition was held to find a name through the local press. The winner of the £5 prize was a lady from North Harrow who came up with Northwood Hills. The Ruislip-Northwood Council wasn't very impressed. It would have preferred Northwood Town. Boards were erected in muddy Joel Street announcing the impending new station, which was opened in December 1933. It was the last of C W Clark's domestic style Metropolitan stations. By then, London Transport was in being. Houses soon began creeping up muddy Porridge Pot Hill, which was renamed Potter Street for suburban tastes. Neal erected long parades of shops. These included W H Smith & Son and the Rex Cinema (erected in 1936). Gas was supplied by the Gas Light & Coke Co, and their steam-driven massive delivery lorries were a familiar sight on the road. Power was provided by a local company, The Northwood Electric Light & Power Company. But the first residents in the chill of winter were not completely happy. After the sophistication of inner London suburbs, they found the pioneer life had disadvantages.

'I arrived at a station,' wrote one early Metro-land pioneer, 'and stepped into mud of the most adhesive quality I had ever seen or felt . . . Yet I was to find that residing in a suburb adds a thrill and a zest to life. It is an experience in having no traditions to live up to.'

The 1934 local Ruislip-Northwood guide book rather overdid things when Northwood Hills was described as being '300ft above sea level and on the borders of Middlesex and Hertfordshire'. A cheap day ticket to take housewives to Baker Street in one of the smart compartment-type electric trains cost 1s 7d (8p) return. Northwood had, of course, been one of the first suburbs on the Metropolitan main line. The Gatehill estate was built between the two World Wars, but much of the area remained wooded or covered by golf courses.

Northwood Hills station opened on Monday, 11th November 1933. Mud and yet more mud was a feature of many suburbs. Shops soon appeared along Joel Street, and there was a cinema which opened in Pinner Road in 1936.

The Metropolitan to Stanmore.

The most rapidly built-up areas of the Underground suburbs were the places along the Metropolitan Railway line to Stanmore. The four mile branch from Wembley Park, with its three intermediate stations, was planned and constructed in a remarkably short space of time. The Metropolitan Railway had often looked northwards from its main line at Wembley Park towards Edgware and even beyond.

The main barrier was raising enough finance. The Government's Development (Loan Guarantees & Grants) Act of 1929 was a scheme to improve trade and reduce unemployment. The Metropolitan very quickly applied for a grant, and its directors decided on a branch to Stanmore. The Metropolitan Railway enabling act was passed on the 4th June 1930.

Despite heavy works involving diversion of the Wealdstone Brook and some deep cuttings in the slippery Middlesex clay, coupled with very wet weather, the line was completed and opened on 10th December 1932. The ceremony was performed by the Minister of Transport, P J Pybus. There was a special train for the VIPs and press, consisting of electric compartment stock, also the saloon carriage known as the Rothschild Saloon.

Outside peak hours, each train consisted of a single electric car with cabs at each end, and there was a total of 144 trains per day. Kingsbury, Canons Park and Stanmore stations were designed by C W Clark in his usual domestic style, first seen on the Watford branch in 1925.

The *Harrow Observer* in December 1932 had a special article on the new line and mentioned that a large firm of builders were already preparing to build a huge estate on the former Stag Lane Aerodrome site, north of Kingsbury. The local newspaper announced a competition to name the new station to serve it and the winning title was 'Queensbury'.

The Queensbury estate was to provide homes for 50,000 people and would be carefully planned, but there would be some light industry. Houses were priced between £600 and £800. Queensbury station was opened on the 16th December 1934, but traffic was slow to develop. This was possibly because the Metropolitan Railway had charged main-line fares, and people found it cheaper to go to Edgware by bus and take the Hampstead (Northern line) tube. Queensbury became the most rapidly developed estate in the north-west segment of London. The landscape was more or less devoid of natural features. Even the few elms were cut down along Honeypot Lane (the 'honey' was probably a reference to the stickiness of the Middlesex mud)!

Stag Lane Aerodrome had been founded by William Warren in 1917 for war training. After the First World War, Amy Johnson learned to fly here for £4 per hour. The De Havilland Aircraft Company also had a plant here and built the famous Tiger Moth. But eventually De Havillands moved their flying operations and part of the factory to Hatfield. By 1934 the land was for sale, and the great estate was begun. The principal developers were Hilbery Chaplin & Co and the Sharon Development Co, with John Laing & Co building the houses. Even as early as December 1932, the plans were being drawn up.

One of the early Laing developments in the area was at Whitchurch Lane, Canons Park, where houses were advertised as being in '*beautifully wooded grounds within a few minutes of the new Canons Park Met Railway Station*'. Queensbury attracted many lower-income families who, before that time, had not been able to afford a home of their own. They came to Queensbury because, like so many others, they wanted something more than to pay high rents all their working lives and have nothing to show for it at the end.

At Queensbury people had a small home with modern conveniences like an Ideal hot water boiler in the kitchenette, a small garden and even a space for a garage. Parades of shops, with some eighty or so units to let, appeared quickly near the station and, if people didn't fancy the daily ride to London, there were local firms setting up in the nearby Honeypot Lane and Edgware Road industrial areas.

At Kingsbury, the Metropolitan Railway station and its flanking shops were soon all but lost in a huge length of shopping parades. There were even two cinemas by the end of the 1930s, and the only open space left was Roe Green Park and the land towards Barn Hill. '*Kingsbury . . . the Queen of North West London suburbs,*' announced one developer. '*There are no steep hills, yet the estate is sufficiently high to give splendid views over the countryside.*' Strangely enough, that stretch of open land has survived on both sides of Fryent Way.

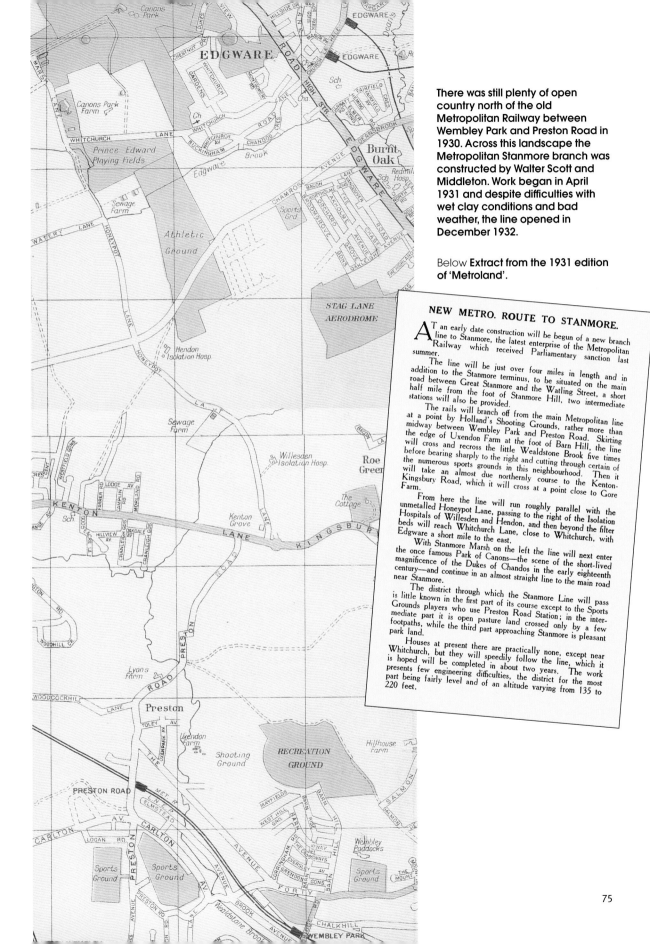

There was still plenty of open country north of the old Metropolitan Railway between Wembley Park and Preston Road in 1930. Across this landscape the Metropolitan Stanmore branch was constructed by Walter Scott and Middleton. Work began in April 1931 and despite difficulties with wet clay conditions and bad weather, the line opened in December 1932.

Below **Extract from the 1931 edition of 'Metroland'.**

NEW METRO. ROUTE TO STANMORE.

AT an early date construction will be begun of a new branch line to Stanmore, the latest enterprise of the Metropolitan Railway which received Parliamentary sanction last summer.

The line will be just over four miles in length and in addition to the Stanmore terminus, to be situated on the main road between Great Stanmore and the Watling Street, a short half mile from the foot of Stanmore Hill, two intermediate stations will also be provided.

The rails will branch off from the main Metropolitan line at a point by Holland's Shooting Grounds, rather more than midway between Wembley Park and Preston Road. Skirting the edge of Uxendon Farm at the foot of Barn Hill, the line will cross and recross the little Wealdstone Brook five times before bearing sharply to the right and cutting through certain of the numerous sports grounds in this neighbourhood. Then it will take an almost due northerly course to the Kenton-Kingsbury Road, which it will cross at a point close to Gore Farm.

From here the line will run roughly parallel with the unmetalled Honeypot Lane, passing to the right of the Isolation Hospitals of Willesden and Hendon, and then beyond the filter beds will reach Whitchurch Lane, close to Whitchurch, with Edgware a short mile to the east.

With Stanmore Marsh on the left the line will next enter the once famous Park of Canons—the scene of the short-lived magnificence of the Dukes of Chandos in the early eighteenth century—and continue in an almost straight line to the main road near Stanmore.

The district through which the Stanmore Line will pass is little known in the first part of its course except to the Sports Grounds players who use Preston Road Station; in the intermediate part it is open pasture land crossed only by a few footpaths, while the third part approaching Stanmore is pleasant park land.

Houses at present there are practically none, except near Whitchurch, but they will speedily follow the line, which it is hoped will be completed in about two years. The work presents few engineering difficulties, the district for the most part being fairly level and of an altitude varying from 135 to 220 feet.

In 1932 Henry J Clarke of Old Church Lane, Kingsbury, advertised his *'Ideal homes estate . . . the new addition to Metro-land . . . artistically designed houses within a few minutes of the two new Metro stations.'* There was also the Audley estate, where *'Happiness means homes of quality and distinction'* which were available on special terms for civil servants and school teachers. F G Parsons & Sons assured purchasers that *'time alone will tell . . . we guarantee our houses'.*

Facing page top **The new Kingsbury station in 1934/5 on the Metropolitan Railway to Stanmore (1932). Sites in the foreground are for the future shopping parades. Across the deep railway cutting, sparkling new 'Tudor' style houses are under construction in Crundale Avenue.**

Facing page bottom **Shops under construction at Queensbury in 1934. In the background on embankment is the Metropolitan.**

Below **A new concrete highway, Cumberland Road, leads to the roundabout in front of Queensbury station in February 1937. The builders Laings are well represented and in the background are the houses of Croxden Close.**

The London Passenger Transport Board's New Works Plan included the project to relieve the twin tracks of the Metropolitan line between Baker Street and Finchley Road by extending the Bakerloo line beneath and running the tube trains on to Wembley Park over two of the Metropolitan's four tracks, then taking over the Metropolitan service to Stanmore.

The first Bakerloo trains ran to Stanmore on the 20th November 1939, with seven trains an hour in peak periods. The old Metropolitan goods yard was closed at Stanmore and replaced by sidings for the Bakerloo trains.

Top **The Stanmore Branch was not long served by the Metropolitan Railway, tube trains on the extension of the Bakerloo line taking over in 1939. Canons Park station was built adjacent to the site of Canons Park Farm, redeveloped for housing in the 1930s.**

Above **Canons Park station soon after it opened in 1932. The suffix 'Edgware' was removed in 1933. The wooden construction of the platforms and plain architecture contrast with the exciting Art Deco style stations of the Piccadilly line built at the same time.**

Left **Stanmore station as opened by the Metropolitan Railway in 1932.** It was served by the Bakerloo line for 40 years to 1979 when it became the northern terminus of the Jubilee line.

Below **Laings 'Jubilee House'** was shown at the 1935 Ideal Homes Exhibition at Olympia and attracted a great deal of interest. A similar house was also built outside King's Cross station to attract Londoners to the green fields of Middlesex. Laings show house and estate office was at the junction of Honeypot Lane and Whitchurch Lane. The jubilee referred to was that of George V, who completed 25 years on the throne in 1935.

LAINGS JUBILEE HOUSE
AT CANONS PARK

Built at the Ideal Home Exhibition 1935, Laings Jubilee House represents the standard of a sensible, comfortable, well planned and well lighted three bedroom house.

Its wonderful De Luxe kitchen will appeal to every woman. The housewife's needs — ample cupboard and larder room; see full description and illustration on page 14 of this booklet.

FREEHOLD PRICES, ETC.

	DETACHED		SEMI-DETACHED	
	Aberdeen (A.)	Rona (R.A.)	Aberdeen (A.)	Rona (R.A.)
Price	£910	£830	£840	£760
Deposit	£80	£70	£60	£50
Approx. Weekly Outgoings :				
To Building Society	24/9	22/9	23/2	21/4
Rates (including Water)	6/2	5/4	5/9	4/10
Total	30/11	28/1	28/11	26/2

Facing Bricks All Round £20 extra.

Approximate Room sizes	Front Reception	Rear Reception	Kitchen	No. 1 Bedroom	No. 2 Bedroom	No. 3 Bedroom
Jubilee Aberdeen (A.)	13' 4" x 11' 2"	16' 5" x 10' 7"	10' 0" x 9' 0"	16' 0" x 10' 10"	14' 3" x 10' 10"	9' 0" x 6' 0"
Jubilee Rona (R.A.) (slightly smaller).	12' 3" x 11' 2"	14' 9" x 10' 7"	9' 9" x 9' 0"	15' 0" x 10' 10"	12' 9" x 10' 10"	8' 5" x 6' 0"

Separate W.C.   Bathroom with marbled-front Bath and Pedestal Lavatory Basin

JOHN LAINGS CONSTRUCTION

The Piccadilly Line to Rayners Lane.

With the completion of the Underground railway improvements between Hammersmith and Acton Town, there were four tracks available. The outer lines were to be used by the District stopping services, the two inner pair for non-stop Piccadilly trains between these two places. The Piccadilly trains ran a full service to South Harrow from 4th July 1932. The running time between Finsbury Park and South Harrow was 45 minutes. On 23rd October 1933, the service was extended over the viaduct to Rayners Lane and on to Uxbridge, providing a joint service with the Metropolitan Railway between the latter two places.

The tube trains looked strangely diminutive standing beside the 'main line' sized Metropolitan saloon or compartment stock. But the passengers soon began to use the tube service and its alternative route to the heart of the West End.

The old Park Royal station was replaced by a station sited on the Western Avenue just to the east of Hanger Lane from the 6th July 1931. The station buildings by Day, Welch & Lander were completed in permanent form in March 1936. The tall tower, with its London Transport symbol, became a conspicuous landmark for local people and the employees of the new factories then being built in that area. Day, Welch & Lander also designed houses on the adjacent Haymills' Hanger Hill estate between 1928 and 1935.

Facing page **The Piccadilly line extensions to the west gave faster journeys on the former District Railway South Harrow branch by cutting out stops between Hammersmith and Acton Town. To handle increased traffic most of the stations north west of Acton Town were rebuilt. Work is shown in progress at Ealing Common.**

Above **The new Park Royal station, Piccadilly line in July 1936, an imposing building dominating the light industrial landscape beside the Western Avenue.**

Below **North Ealing: Corringway – a typical suburban road, with plenty of space to park the family car and grow roses. North Ealing station was a short walk away at the southern end and Park Royal at the northern end.**

Old Alperton & Perivale station from Ealing Road. It opened in 1903 and was a favourite place for visitors to the canal and sparkling river Brent. The building on the right is the old Baptist chapel. Clifford Sabey and other builders quickly covered the area between Alperton and Wembley from 1925 onwards.

Alperton station was rebuilt in 1931, and a bus garage was erected next door in June 1939. But it was the next station, Sudbury Town, that was important as the style setter (or prototype) for the new generation of Holden stations. It was completed in July 1931. Its lofty booking hall, with tall windows, its bronze lamp fittings and its illuminated station name (since removed) were much admired. There was an ample turning space for buses outside and even provision for a café.

In this view of Greenford Road at Sudbury Hill, the old wooden District Railway station building can be seen on the left.

Sudbury Hill and South Harrow were also rebuilt. At South Harrow the new station was sited by the shopping centre in Northolt Road, the buildings being below the Roxeth Viaduct. Once again, there was a bus turning space. The inhabitants of the long rows of new terraced houses at Northolt Park, Northolt, and along the seemingly interminable Whitton Avenue (constructed in 1934) from Sudbury, could hop on a bus and be taken straight to the tube stations along the line rather than use the old-fashioned and sooty steam trains of the LNER Marylebone line – Sudbury Hill (Harrow) station and Sudbury (Harrow Road) – or Northolt on the Great Western Railway.

The quiet and flat countryside near South Harrow, with Harrow Hill rising majestically to the north, attracted day trippers from early District Railway days. Northolt Road was a pleasant country road, and thousands of children and adults visited The Paddocks, not far from the present-day Alexandra Avenue and also Northolt Park station. At

The Paddocks were thirty acres of grounds full of attractions such as roundabouts, donkey rides, see-saws, picnic areas and a miniature railway. When the tea gardens finally closed, part of the land was incorporated into the new Alexandra Park.

As late as 1931 the area remained fairly rural, and purchasers of new houses were told: '*The visitor with a love for picturesque houses will be pleased with the charming dairy farmhouse not far from the station on the Northolt Road; cream-washed and many gabled, gay with borders of well-formed flowers and climbing roses . . .*'.

Piecemeal development along the 'Long Mile', which was renamed Eastcote Lane, began in the mid-1920s. Eventually, the vast T F Nash Rayners Lane estate was to link up at a number of places from the early 1930s onwards. Other builders were also hard at work, covering every square foot of meadow land, felling every tree they could get their saws across, until they finally achieved complete coverage of the landscape.

The new Sudbury Hill station opened in 1932. It is seen here with a row of typical suburban shops shortly after the end of the Second World War. The modern station contrasted with the LNER station, Sudbury Hill (Harrow), a few hundred yards along Greenford Road to the right.

Westward to Hounslow.

The extension of the Piccadilly line over the District tracks to Hounslow was through an area that had been comparatively undisturbed in the immediate post-First World War period. The District branch had run through flat fields and market gardens for much of its route to Hounslow. But plans were being put in hand for a modern trunk road that would bypass the traffic bottlenecks of Brentford and Hounslow and take the growing motor traffic directly out towards Staines and north Surrey. This arterial highway, called the Great West Road, had been an idea as far back as the early 1900s – one of its instigators was Lord Montagu of Beaulieu, the motoring pioneer. The Great West Road (1925) encouraged ribbon development of generally high-class housing.

The road was revolutionary for England at that time, with provision for cycle tracks – the forerunner of the separated traffic systems of modern towns. Served both by District and Piccadilly trains and, in addition, by the new road, the areas of Syon and Osterley quickly filled up.

In 1935 Hounslow seemed to be hardly aware of the new role that the age of the common man had cast upon it – the service area of a vast dormitory linked to London. The old High Street was still lined by comfortable old inns and quaint shops, although a couple of old drapers' businesses were then modernising to offer complete house furnishing departments. They were Edmonds (Bon Marché) and Murfitts. Between them was a bustle of tiny grocers' and hardware shops, with the stores of old-established grocery chains like David Greig, Maypole (where butter could be knocked up with wooden bats and impressed with a pattern selected by the customer), and Star International – full of flavours and aromas of the East.

Outside, the electric trams hurried by to take home those people who lived in the older districts of Isleworth and Busch Corner. The trams were soon replaced by smart new trolleybuses, which swept by to their new terminus further along the Staines Road. Here a special turning circle had been constructed for them at 'The Wellington' public house.

The tremendous impact of housing development west of Hounslow came with the extension of the Piccadilly line service. Two additional tracks were constructed between Turnham Green and Northfields, and the work was completed on 18th December 1932. A full service of Piccadilly trains worked to Northfields from 9th January 1933, and a huge new depot was constructed there. The final pre-war extension of this branch was achieved when a full service to Hounslow West station began on 13th March 1933. Between 1933 and the outbreak of the Second World War, all the land between the Hounslow West terminus and Harlington (with the exception of some pockets) was built over. The stations along the Hounslow line were improved at this time, with a keen appreciation of the linking role between car, bus and train.

The old District Railway station known as Osterley & Spring Grove was closed in March 1934, and a modern Underground station called Osterley was erected at the intersection of the new Great West Road, half-a-mile westwards. The new stations at Osterley (with its illuminated tower) and Hounslow West looked their best at night, the illuminated fascias and dome of Hounslow West station being visible for some distance.

Although passengers at Hounslow East had a miserable wait on their draughty and exposed platform until the new waiting room and canopy were put up in 1965, by the summer of 1933 the Hounslow services offered fast trains both by District and Piccadilly line trains. They linked the new commuters living west of Hounslow to the centre of London within 40 minutes or so. By then, all of the market gardens and orchards were disappearing at an ever accelerating rate under bricks and mortar.

It was still possible, even after 1934, to step outside Hounslow West station and very soon walk in semi-countryside. By the 1930s most of the land between Hounslow Town and the Barracks had been built over; but a broad band of pasture stretched unbroken towards the junction with the new Great West Road, with the exception of a Victorian cottage, which suffered a direct hit by one of the first V2 rockets in the Second World War.

The land that bordered the northern side of the Bath Road was under market garden cultivation. This area was about to be built over as the Second World War began (the builders' huts were then used as a greengrocers, selling produce from the land immediately behind it).

Above **Chiswick Park District Railway station is a good mile from Chiswick Park House! Here is the station being rebuilt in 1932, with a temporary booking office. Charles Holden designed the new building with its distinctive drum-shaped tower so that it was conspicuous from Chiswick High Road.**

Below left **The old station at Northfields & Little Ealing, with the premises of Ealing District Steam Laundry to the left. The original halt opened on the 16th April 1908, but was rebuilt as seen here in 1911. Little Ealing and Northfields districts were mainly built up by 1914. One of the late Victorian residents was Charles Blondin, who lived at Niagara House between 1886 and 1897. He was the celebrated tight-rope walker over the Niagara Falls.**

Below right **The new Northfields station opened on a new site to an admiring public in October 1933. It was designed by Stanley Heaps, but much influenced by Charles Holden. It must have been a remarkable shock to the older residents of this sedate part of Ealing.**

It was possible to rent a newly built home within a short distance of Hounslow High Street in 1933 for 24/- (£1.20) per week. These houses had three bedrooms, separate WC and even a garage space. But most of the young working-class couples were interested in owning their houses – the start of what was more recently called 'a property owning democracy'. The rented houses were often, in fact, sited on parts of the estate which had not been successfully sold off, the choice for prospective buyers being practically limitless, with so many estates springing up. During 1934 alone, 35,000 houses had been built in the Metropolitan Water Board area, and house building was to break all records with the improved Underground services to Hounslow.

To the north, around Heston, R T Warren was erecting houses which soon gained a good reputation for quality. Warren was also building farther north at Hillingdon and Ickenham, Hayes and Uxbridge. His slogan was: 'Take a form of security in bricks and mortar'. His houses in the Heston area in March 1933 sold for £525 freehold in Cranford Lane. In 1935 in the immediate vicinity of Hounslow West station the last few houses were for sale by G T Crouch on the site of a lovely old orchard. Crouch-built houses were good standard semi-detached, at a time when more and more terraced houses (in blocks of four or six) were being erected to secure a lower individual selling price. They were decorated with mock-Tudor timbering and had leaded glass in bays overlooking the main road, albeit at a respectable distance. A Crouch house cost £799 and included garage space. Few of the new houses actually boasted garages which would have raised the purchase price. In any event house buyers were not expected to be able to afford to run a car as well as to repay their mortgage. But 'garage space' was sought by many forward-looking purchasers with an eye to the rising popularity of the motor-car.

W J Harris was, arguably, the biggest builder in the Hounslow West area. He swept away the flat acres of orchard and market garden (with the occasional gravel pit) that stretched beckoningly westward.

Cressy Corner. Hounslow, 1.

First he built around the immediate station area before spreading westwards towards the road to Cranford. On the south side of the Bath Road, Harris developed his extensive Cranford Manor estate, which at one time threatened to reach south as far as the Great South West Road. This was another arterial road, and was really an extension of the Great West Road. In the previous ten years Harris had been responsible for building over 2,000 houses around Hounslow. They were of terraced design, with slate damp courses and small variations in style from block to block, mostly in regard to exterior decoration. There were assorted porches, different coloured glass in the front door panels, and several different designs of wooden fencing separating the houses. End-of-terrace houses (which shared a driveway to give 'garage space') were priced at £575 freehold in 1935, whilst others in the block went at £550 and £565.

These Harris houses were well built with brick partition walls between rooms, quarry-tiled kitchens (which were fitted with a dresser and a gas copper). The builder offered a choice of colours for tiled fire-surrounds, and interiors were decorated according to the buyers' choice, although they were warned to choose 'plain wallpapers'.

Harris also built a public house (The Berkeley Arms) and parade of shops fronting the Bath Road. These, surprisingly, were designed in French chateau style, sporting round towers and pretty blue-grey roof tiles. But in the centre of the parade was something even more startling: a petrol station with a thatched roof!

Nearer Cranford village arose the more splendid 'semis' built by Laing from 1933 onwards. These were priced at some £200 above Harris's price, but were built on more generous plots. At this point, the Underground terminus was well over twenty minutes' walk away; but developers continued to

Left **A corner of the Old Hounslow just off the busy High Street in the early 1920s. The area around the old Middlesex coaching town grew rapidly in the 1930s, particularly after Piccadilly trains were extended along the District Railway in 1933.**

A typical shopping parade and cinema at Hounslow. The Dominion cinema opened in 1931 and closed in 1961. The new Tudor-style shops and the public house were some of the amenities for new residents. On Saturday nights there were two films plus live artistes, such as Herman Darewiski and his band.

exploit the virgin land up to and even beyond the river Crane. There were similar developments due north of Hounslow West station towards Heston.

W Grenville Collins started his Cranford Cross estate in this area with even lower prices in 1936, advertising homes from as little as £420 or 10/3d (51p) per week. For those house buyers who sought to work in London, a long cycle ride or walk to Hounslow West station stared them grimly in the face as the penalty for buying such cheap contentment.

It would have been strange indeed if this complete change to the face of West Middlesex which happened during the course of twenty years or so was able to take place without some sadness: perhaps by those who took up the promise of a new house away from London grime but were unable to keep up their mortgage repayments when the Great Depression of the 1930s put many workers on short time or forced them out of a job altogether; or perhaps by nature lovers and those lamenting the lost pastoral pleasure that Middlesex had once offered, and which Sir John Betjeman voiced in his poetic trip to the borders of the county *where a few surviving hedges keep alive our lost Elysium – rural Middlesex again*.

Piccadilly to Cockfosters.

Before penetration by the Underground, the country north of London was served by the unreliable steam rail services of the Great Northern Railway (LNER from 1923), by electric trams, and later by the aggressively expanding bus services.

In the Barnet area, a local horse-drawn cab service, run by a Mr Parsloe, easily dealt with local traffic from the two Barnet stations up to the little town, surrounded as it was by fields and hedgerows. Some development had taken place around the town, and this gradually spread beside the main road connections to London. But away to the east, the country consisted of a number of quite large estates including Arnos Grove and Osidge (owned by Sir Thomas Lipton, the Victorian tea magnate) which, together with Oak Hill Park and Monkfrith, made a solid slab of private green amid the farmlands between East Barnet and Southgate villages.

The Underground's Piccadilly line, which was to open up this area in the 1930s, had had its northern terminus at Finsbury Park since 1906. The Great Northern Railway, which owned Finsbury Park station, viewed the Underground line as nothing other than a feeder for its own services to Barnet, Hatfield and Welwyn. However, other plans had been formulated by an American banker, John Pierpoint Morgan who, as early as 1902, had formed a syndicate to build new tube railways, including a line from Hammersmith out to Southgate, then little more than a huddle of cottages, a smithy, a church and a chapel.

This brought Morgan into direct confrontation with his compatriot, Charles Tyson Yerkes, who was also promoting a scheme to build a line from Hammersmith. The success of the Morgan proposals hinged on co-operation with London United Tramways, whose plans for tubes around Hammersmith and beyond were crucial to the entire complex receiving parliamentary approval. At the last moment, to the consternation of the Morgan party, Yerkes and his associates acquired the LUT interest. Consequently, the Morgan proposals no longer represented the scheme which Parliament had provisionally sanctioned, so Morgan was forced to withdraw from the contest.

For High Barnet, Underground rail services were to prove very slow in coming. In fact, it was only dur-

ing the Second World War that the line was electrified. But until something could be agreed about the Finsbury Park problem, the north London proposals towards Southgate were also 'in the air' and could have ended up with the same timescale as Barnet.

Under an Act of August 1902 the proposals north of Finsbury Park were abandoned and the company, now the Great Northern, Piccadilly & Brompton Railway, went ahead with work in west London to a terminus at Hammersmith. Unfortunately, with the abandonment of powers, an agreement with the Great Northern became operative under which future extensions could only by carried out with Great Northern consent.

However, by the end of the First World War, the public clamour for something to be done about the bad travelling conditions for north London commuters began to gather momentum. It was no good having a home if it could not be reached easily after work and enjoyed. And, of course, the working hours in those days were longer, so that the travel problems, which became increasingly abundant, could not be eased away by the staggering of working times.

The press of those days, as indeed today, saw good reporting material in this popular daily misery of movement. The *Daily Mirror* press campaign at the end of 1922 certainly led the public outcry for an extension of the Underground line from Finsbury Park, and the minister concerned had to face a large number of public deputations from the Finsbury Park area, each having the same tale of distress to tell, as workers fought to board trams and buses for the homeward journey. Men and women, it was said, had to fight in rugby-type scrums for a place on the vehicles. And, whilst this was going on, pickpockets fell upon the unfortunate people. Working with a skill that could be likened to that of the present day, the agitators sought the help of doctors to describe the nervous conditions that seemed to strike at the prettiest women, whilst others spoke of the diseases of the chest that took many a man, who had survived the trenches of Flanders, to an early grave.

However, when an MP was able to say that he had been knocked down himself whilst attempting to board a tram at Finsbury Park, Parliament stirred

Old Southgate – a scene at the Green in about 1920, with buses to Victoria on route 29. The Cherry Tree Inn and other ancient and attractive buildings here formed the heart of old Southgate. The name of the village is derived from the 'south gate' to Enfield Chase. The Walker family of nearby Arnos Grove (1777–1918) instigated cricket here, and John Walker founded Southgate Cricket Club in 1855. The family was also instrumental in establishing the MCC at Lords in 1877.

itself more effectively, especially when faced with a petition of some 30,000 signatures. This was presented in June 1923, after it became known that the Underground Group had removed its interest to south London because of the obstructive attitude of the London & North Eastern Railway, based on the long-lamented agreement which had been made with its predecessor. A Public Enquiry was called for before the London & Home Counties Traffic Advisory Committee.

The Report, which appeared on the 17th March 1926, indicated that there was a clear case for action to be taken: a train service from north and north-east London into the West End. It also suggested that an extension of the Underground was an obvious step. As a matter of urgency the Piccadilly line should be extended to Manor House and, the Report continued, a further extension should be constructed to Wood Green and, if possible, even to Southgate.

Witnesses who had appeared before the Committee had suggested that there was no cause to fear competition between the main line trains of the LNER and new Underground trains, as the main line had the advantage of higher speeds to attract business from areas farther away from London. Also, it was planned to take the Underground extension away from the line of route of the main line. In this way, the Underground, when it did arrive, sliced through acres of fields to Cockfosters on the Hertfordshire border.

The London & North Eastern and its predeces-

sors had generally neglected their suburban lines for decades, a practice that had gained momentum during the war years. Those passengers who were forced to use its trains complained of their being irregular, and letters to the press spoke often of the poor standard of service. The Report, therefore, was generally welcomed, none more so than by a number of astute estate agents and developers who had already smelt big profits for the taking, after pleasant experiences in the Hendon and Finchley areas before the First World War.

However, there was the usual delay when it came to discovering who was to pay for such a laudable scheme. It was not until 1929, in fact, under the Labour Government of Ramsay MacDonald that the Development (Loan Guarantees and Grants) Act enabled the capital at last to be raised for the extension of the Piccadilly line in north and west London. The extension to Southgate was the single biggest item qualifying for grant. There was every hope that there would be no further opposition from the LNER. However, this was soon to be shattered when Sir Ralph Wedgwood, for the main line company, opposed the proposal for the Southgate extension on the ground that the company conjectured that there would be a loss of £100,000 a year through the reduction of interchange passengers flowing through Finsbury Park. Indeed, the company was alarmed at the turn of events and proposed that it should electrify its own line to Welwyn, with branches serving High Barnet and Edgware.

The Bill, however, was not delayed on this account, for this was a time when attempts were being made to deal with London's transport needs from a comprehensive viewpoint, paving the way for the formation of the London Passenger Transport Board only a few years later, and Parliament was successful in placing pressure on the LNER.

During the building of the extension from Finsbury Park, there was much local pressure (common when a new tube is being built) for a local station, and especially the distance of about 1.5 miles between Manor House and Turnpike Lane was raised, with a request for an intermediate station. Frank Pick, the Underground's Vice Chairman and main promoter of the scheme, refused this. In his view, any station should serve as an interchange for bus and tram routes; but between these two stations the trains would run parallel with road services, and he saw no point in a station which would have little interchange possibilities.

The Underground stations were given great planning care, with Frank Pick taking a very direct and central role. He was able to write to his Chief Engineer about Turnpike Lane, completed in Spring 1933 (although it had been open for the previous eight months): 'I am pleased with the . . . station now it is completed. The subways are an improvement on [those] previously built. Altogether we have . . . a credit to our undertaking'.

It was, of course, at the far end of the new line where land was cheapest and where developers and new house buyers had most to gain. The Great Depression had hardly lifted, yet the misery did bring cheap labour, and, in London, a gradually increasing optimism had promoted the feeling of a great new age. It gave everyone just a hint of intoxication after the dreary reminders of the horrors of war. In north London, as elsewhere around the capital, the message was the same – get out to the fields and bird song! It was missing the point for a columnist of the *Palmers Green & Southgate Gazette* to pontificate: '*The young married couple of today prefers a small flat more to their taste, and are loath to burden themselves with a large house. I visited a new home of two young friends the other day and was amazed to see how comfortable and spacious only two rooms can be if they have been cleverly furnished*'.

Most Londoners had had enough of rooms, and the prospect of a new house, at little more than the rent for two rooms nearer Town, meant that the estate developers had no great selling problem other than over-supply by the mid-thirties.

The construction of the tube railway was able to move apace when the area round the new Arnos Grove station was reached, for the new line was then to run on the surface mainly through a rural stretch, although there was a tunnel under Southgate. Trees

Constructing Cockfosters terminus for the Piccadilly line extension in 1933. The architect was Charles Holden. The design was later adapted for the new terminus at Uxbridge in 1938.

were cut, ancient hedges felled, and the rattle of contractors' wagons brought such an air of excitement that the prim local council was prepared to look with affability at the planning requests that arrived for further housing projects.

In 1932 before the proposed date for the opening of the extension from Arnos Grove to Enfield West on the 13th March 1933, there were houses going up at The Birches, directly overlooking Oakwood Park, for £1,115 freehold – a considerable sum for those days, and an indication of the high-class type of housing which was being built.

When the Enfield West and Southgate sections opened, public excitement reached fever pitch. The air was heady with talk of the new London Passenger Transport Board which was planned to take over in the following July, and the 'brave new world' image infected everyone. It was reported that the railway on opening day had issued 30,000 free tickets for use after 10 am, and that all but a few had been used.

There were also special facilities for the people from Hounslow and district to visit the new extension from Arnos Grove to Enfield West and, throughout the day, there were packed trains arriving from the west. Many had held the same opinion as a letter writer in the local press who had complained, during the previous month, of the deplorable conditions on the LNER suburban services in these terms:

Sir, I wonder whether the governing board of the suburban services of the LNER will look into the travelling conditions that regular passengers and season ticket holders experience daily. The dirt on the carriages is common knowledge, but until recently there had been some effort to keep them clean, at least for 1st class passengers. Now they are uncomfortable and cold. I instance the 9.19, with a change at Finsbury Park into a Moorgate train that is even colder still. There are many who say that the quicker the whole of the railway becomes another branch of the tube, the better it will be for all of us.

The press and media generally vied with each other for descriptive intoxication. Someone had said that the site of the new Enfield West station was the highest point in Europe, if a straight line were drawn, until the Urals were reached. When challenged on this, the newspaper said that it was given information by 'one of the Underground engineers at the site'. The publicity authorities of the Underground responded by shifting the credit to Cockfosters.

A magazine article of February 1934 commenting on the new Southgate station stated: 'The traffic is beginning to grow, and 750 houses are included in the programme to midsummer for the district. It is expected that Southgate will become one of the most important stations on the extension.'

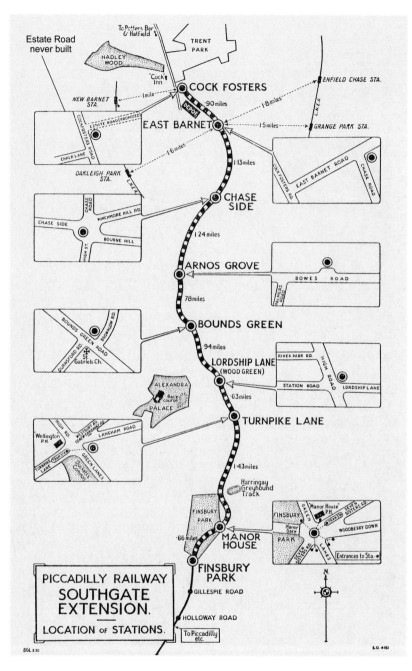

A press advert and a poster for the Cockfosters extension of the Piccadilly line. The press advert, dated March 1930, shows earlier planned names for three of the stations and the spelling of the terminus station as two words.

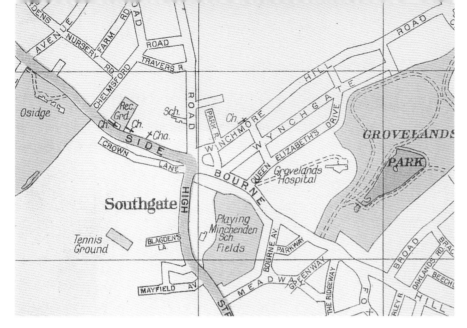

Southgate Village and its surroundings in 1930. The Piccadilly line station was built at the junction of Crown Lane and Chase Side two years later. Much of the area was then built up, but Grovelands Park survives.

Southgate under construction in 1932. Work began on the tube station on 22nd June 1931. This picture is full of contrasts: the old horse trough and the cottages against the fresh appeal of Charles Holden's tube station. The provisional name of the station had been Chase Side, the road on the right. Half way along the street on the right were the offices of Hugh Davies, a famous name in the inter-War development of both the Southgate and Golders Green areas. By 1939 Chase Side had changed into a typical suburban shopping street.

Cockfosters station was opened on 31st July 1933 and the first Monday in August was a Bank Holiday in those days, hence the press advert, left.
In the poster below, the minimal depiction of the LNER main line is of note.

By the end of April 1934, news came about that the new transport authority had re-considered the name of Enfield West station, which was nearly 2 miles from Enfield town. The LPTB had decided to avoid any confusion by adding in brackets after the name Enfield West the word 'Oakwood'. Residents were assured that in a very short time this new name would be a regular district name for the area.

Sure enough, the new district was not long in getting established. There had been limited development in the area during the early 1920s, but nothing to compare with the mass of bricks and mortar that started to flow over the open fields with the coming of the tube. The position of Enfield West station was for some months in the middle of 'wide open spaces' and, as the roads for the new houses cut through hedges and fields, the local big estates were being swept away. Thirty London firms were developing the Southgate estate in 1934, with Davies Hampden Way estate houses going for £695. The Ideal Housing Company, also at work, strove to sell its dearer houses with the advertisement that was 'inserted to catch the eye of prospective purchasers who are willing to purchase a house for £1,000'.

Local Town Planning attempted to control the spread of housing in an ordered way 'to preserve health and the amenities, as more and more people are choosing Southgate for the first time, where the land offers so much that is still blissful and remote'. But it was to be remote for only a very short time, as housing ('no cheap and nasty project allowed') swept out from the stations. In Southgate at this time there were already 1,000 houses and, by 1935, the public were told that there would be double that number. Few voices were raised for the preservation of rural life – all was in the name of progress. As one writer in the area put it in 1934:

'Taking a stroll in any direction . . . one is amazed at the progress made. Rural life has ceased at the hands of the builder; pleasant walks have been replaced by trim roads, many of which have not yet been completed. The old stile by Osidge Lane stands as a pathetic reminder of lost days. One wonders how many troths were plighted there. The axeman has got to work with his axe, and the sound and snort of mechanical excavators in Osidge Lane make it a shadow of its former self.'

COCKFOSTERS STN
OPENS 31ST JULY
Into new country by UNDERGROUND
PICCADILLY LINE
THROUGH TRAINS FROM PICCADILLY

Looking down Prince George's Avenue, Oakwood, in the late 1930s. Builders in the area included Laing, whose South Lodge estate was under construction from 1935 onwards: 'Houses within a few minutes of undulating country and yet within a stone's throw of the tube station.' Oakwood station opened in March 1933 as Enfield West. There was a great deal of discussion on what to call the new station and the surrounding area: Merryhill; Southgate North; Oakwood Park and East Barnet were some of the suggestions.

The Osidge Lane development, announced in 1934, was touched with a certain amount of romantic grandeur, for the estate was the brain-child of a 29 year old man called Hugh Davies who had worked his way up the estate manager's profession just at the right time, founding his own estate agency in Southgate in 1933 and employing a staff of three people. He had previously spent seven years working for the established firm of P H Edwards, operating in Golders Green, Kenton and Mill Hill. Hugh Davies also created London & Suburban Homesteads Ltd to develop land in this area. By the start of the Second World War, he employed some 400 staff in north and south London.

His Osidge Lane development was large – over £1,000,000 changed hands with the purchase of this large slice of land around Sir Thomas Lipton's mansion , just 'up the road' from the new Southgate station. Care was taken to give a sense of spacious-ness to the web of residential roads that sprung up here, and to make sure that, with few exceptions, roads did not lead directly through the area so that the blissful traffic-free nature of life which had hitherto existed around Osidge Lane could be allowed to continue as far as practicable.

But, as always, where money could be made, things moved too fast for comfort. More and more people, many carrying their copy of the EVENING STANDARD 'GUIDE TO HOUSE PURCHASE', were on their way out to Southgate and to Cockfosters, making the clamour for land louder and more insistent. The guide gave helpful hints on everything from the servant problem to roof coverings and boundaries, from mortgages to drains. 'Don't become alarmed if cracks appear in your ceiling,' the book said sooth-ingly, adding that 'the wise householder will endeavour to trace the water supply from stop valve to storage tank' – a hint that proved very timely in those days of lead pipes and winter 'freeze ups' in the unprotected roof space.

During the rest of the 1930s the Cockfosters extension of the Piccadilly line saw the remorseless removal of the surviving landed estates and parks. Two years after the Osidge development, there came the sale of the Monkfrith estate in 1936 just to the north of it. It was advertised as '50 acres of really major building land at a time when there is very little land for building purposes in the district'. This sale was inevitably followed by the sale in the ensuing year of the adjacent estate, that of Bohum Lodge, an oddly-shaped piece of land just to the south of Cat Hill and closer to Cockfosters than Southgate. It realised some £75,000, a very large sum for those days. Here it was planned to build eight houses to the acre.

In 1938 a surviving piece of land known as Oakwood Park, near Southgate station, provided more houses whilst, in the same year, the Southgate estate of Laing, the developers, offered houses of high standard and of very contemporary design for around £1,140 – almost double the price of houses on more mundane estates in London. With Laing, there was the luxury of fitted kitchens. Although 'compact', there were folding seats and a put-away ironing board – and the windows had leaded lights. On Laing's Southgate North estate, which was claimed in a flush of exuberance to be the 'most beautiful . . . in north London', the Jubilee style house was advertised at £995, whilst the Coronation type, with its prominent 'Odeon' inspired rounded entrance, was priced at £1,140. The estate went up some three minutes' walk from Southgate and close to the open land of Trent Park.

All around the new houses of Arnos Grove, Southgate, Cockfosters and Barnet was the promise of every type of amenity: schools, trains ('about every minute' to Town), picnics, golf courses, easy shopping and, of course, cinemas and dance halls, for such places were the temples of health and happiness in the 1930s.

Developments on the Bakerloo Line.

Development along the line from Wembley was slow at first. Industry first appeared at North Wembley during the First World War with the opening of Hooper & Company's aircraft factory in 1916 and British Oxygen in 1918. Wrigley's Chewing Gum opened a factory in 1926. So far as housing was concerned, Wembley Hill Estates had started site development before 1914, and Wembley was already a rather large suburb by the time of the British Empire Exhibition in 1924–25.

Wembley Hill Garden Suburb was advertised in 1933 with 'houses of superior appearance and built of carefully selected materials by Messrs Callow & Wright. Only five minutes from Wembley Bakerloo Tube.' The main shopping centre was well established by the late 1920s, and trams had run through to Sudbury from 1910 (trolleybuses from 1936).

But at North Wembley not all was industry. At South Kenton, where a station was opened on the 3rd July 1933 on the Bakerloo/LMS lines, there were some high-class neo-Tudor housing estates. 'After the toil and stuffiness of the City, you will appreciate the bracing air of this beautiful, healthy suburb. Perfect sanitation.' Comben & Wakeling had already built some 1,500 houses by 1937. Similar houses by F & C Costin – '. . . distinctive Tudor residences of quality . . .' – were also popular in this area. 'When buying a house one cannot make the decision too carefully,' they advised in their brochure. The glossy pages had artists' impressions of their detached and semi-detached houses, with names such as 'The Waverley', 'The Dorchester' and 'The Mayfair' from £780.

At Kenton, Costin were also active. Another developer was H R & P (London) Ltd, who built on the flat fields around Christchurch Avenue and Kenton Lane. The land had at one time been owned by St Bartholomew's Hospital in the City. From about 1928 H R & P had an estate office near Kenton station, and to clients who were doubtful about the wisdom of living over one and a half miles from a railway station, they emphasised that their houses were of good construction and tasteful design. The semi-detached types ranged from £825 and had shared drives for future garages.

The estate spread north almost to Belmont which grew rapidly and soon had parades of shops arranged around a circle and even a cinema, The Essoldo.

Outside Kenton station in 1934. The prominent advertising boards announce freehold houses ranging from £595 to £2,000. One of the signs is for HR&P Estates, who built off Christchurch Avenue – Oakfield, Larkfield and Hartford Avenues. On the right of the picture, behind the workmen is J Warner, the florist. This was a popular place of call for commuting husbands late home from the office!

By the late 1930s Costins were building on the last available pieces of land in Kenton and were offering slightly cheaper homes (see advert opposite).

Centre left Just over the LMS bridge the sign on the right is not for the Underground, but for the showrooms of the North-Met Electricity Supply Co. The premises later became the offices of *The Gramophone* magazine. The parade of shops stretch eastward along Kenton road towards the now long gone Odeon Cinema. Just beyond the shops on the right is Draycott Avenue leading to Woodcock Hill and Northwick Park Circle.

Bottom left Wealdstone with the War Memorial Clock (dedicated by Lt Gen Ironside on the 11th November 1923). The house behind it was Ravenscroft, the home of Dr Butler, local medical officer. Over to the left by the ST type bus is the Wealdstone Cinema – opened in about 1909 as the *Parisian Bioscope*.

Wealdstone was built up in the late nineteenth century, but the slopes of Harrow Weald remained the property of New College, Oxford, until the beginning of the 1930s. Then the College sold, and John Searcy & Co began to develop the New College Estate, with the roads named after historical personalities connected with New College.

Standard Estates built at the northern end of Kenton Lane in 1933, and the builder of the houses, a man named Jefferies, would go round on a Sunday, when people came to visit the site, and offer to lend them the £5 deposit money! 'Houses on gently moulded hills, surrounded by verdant lanes and age-old trees, giving quiet, pastoral beauty. This is the ideal setting for one's home.' Even today some of this sylvan beauty remains.

Hatch End remained fairly open until the late 1930s, and is still surrounded by Green Belt land. 'Hatch End,' remarked a guide book of the late 1920s, 'is one of those very beautiful districts with quite distinctive claims as a delightful and very desirable area. The surrounding countryside is both undulating and well wooded.'

6
SUNSET OF THE SUBURBS

'The neighbourhood of Finchley is charmingly wooded and on every site tall elm trees and silver birches form picturesque backgrounds to delightful views', wrote one imaginative estate developer a century ago. There were a number of large houses, including that of H C Stephens, MP for Hornsey and celebrated ink manufacturer. He gave Victoria Park to the people of Finchley to commemorate Queen Victoria's Diamond Jubilee in 1897. His house is now a museum devoted to the history of pens and writing.

In the nineteenth century, Finchley consisted of three settlements: Church End, North End and East End. The Great North Road ran through Church End and on to Whetstone and High Barnet, across the Middlesex border into Hertfordshire. Barnet was not only famed for its old coaching inns, but also for the Battle of 1471 which was actually fought at nearby Hadley. By the end of the Victorian era there were significant patches of suburban development – mainly along the main road northwards.

The High Barnet and Edgware GNR steam lines provided services to King's Cross, Broad Street and Moorgate; but the poorly maintained and uncomfortable trains were subject to frequent delays, especially in foggy weather. Although houses were built alongside the line at Nether Street and Woodside Park, it was the coming of the Metropolitan Electric Trams (1905–07) to Finchley via Whetstone and on to Barnet that provided services to tube stations such as Golders Green.

After the First World War development proceeded slowly compared with other areas, but there was sufficient commuter traffic for the LNER to open an additional station at West Finchley between Church End and Woodside Park on 1st March 1933.

One of the more ambitious developers was F J Ingram, who developed the land west of Dollis Brook from 1932 onwards, naming his roads after famous landmarks of Sussex. Well built semi-detached houses were available from £975. There were playing fields and public greens along the winding Dollis Brook, with the added attraction of open country to the north.

The London Transport New Works Programme of 1935–40 contained elaborate plans for the extension of the Northern line over the old LNER steam branches. It was intended for the Northern line to be extended beyond Edgware to Bushey Heath via Brockley Hill and Elstree.

The lines to Alexandra Palace via Muswell Hill and Cranley Gardens, and from Finsbury Park to Highgate via Stroud Green and Crouch End were also to become part of the Northern line scheme. The existing line was to be extended from Highgate (now named Archway) to surface at East Finchley LNER, whence tube trains would run over the existing lines to Barnet via Church End, and to Edgware and Bushey Heath via Mill Hill.

By the later part of the 1930s, and in anticipation of the arrival of the Northern line trains to Finchley, Barnet, Mill Hill and Edgware, a number of new housing developments got under way. F J Ingram expanded his estate at Woodside Park west of the Dollis Brook and other developers began to erect houses on the steep slopes above Mill Hill East station. There was also some new development at Mill Hill. However, new developments were on a more modest scale towards Totteridge and Barnet. The supply of houses was reaching what we now call 'market saturation'; then there was the darkening shadow of impending war.

However, the Underground was at last to become reality. Work was well advanced by 1939, and the first section from Highgate to East Finchley was opened on 3rd July 1939. Barnet via Church End (renamed Finchley Central) followed on 14th July 1939. It was an ambitious plan and was welcomed by the long-suffering commuters of Finchley and Barnet. High Barnet followed on 14th April 1940. The final opening was that between Finchley Central and Mill Hill East on 18th May 1941, serving the important barracks. But as the Second World War began to take its toll of manpower and supplies, all further work to the line ceased, never to be resumed.

The Town & Country Planning Act of 1947 facilitated the establishment of a Green Belt which secured ministerial approval in 1954–1959, and included many areas bought for building development before 1940. This led to a re-assessment of traffic predictions, and the result was said to justify abandonment of the unbuilt sections of the pre-War scheme for the Northern line. Over the years there has been much speculation and regret that the intended works were not completed. But one wonders if the scheme was far too complicated to have worked satisfactorily. Trains could have become intolerably overcrowded, passengers confused by the complicated services, and frequent delays might have arisen.

The late 1930s saw builders such as Laing at work on the steep lands around Mill Hill Park: Bittacy Hill and Engle Park, for example. The Parkside estate was advertised as being 'situated upon high, healthy ground, famed for beauty and freshness'. This estate was sited just north of Bunns Lane and near Wise Lane. Today Finchley and Mill Hill still have some pleasant countryside nearby, spared the density of the earlier Underground suburbs.

Highgate LNER station in June 1937 with an LMS train from Broad Street emerging from Highgate Wood tunnel. When the Second World War broke out in 1939, works were well advanced on the rebuilding of what was to be the 'upper' station for the proposed Northern line service from Finsbury Park via Crouch End.

Central Line Extensions.

Plans to extend the Central London trains over the Great Western Railway's proposed Ealing & Shepherd's Bush Railway were put into operation after the First World War. The London County Council at this time began building its vast Wood Lane estate west of White City, and the new tube extension was to include a wooden halt at East Acton to serve the estate. The line was officially opened to the public on the 3rd August 1920, with a lunch for the press and the directors.

The rapid growth of this part of London in the 1920s resulted in two further stations being opened: North Acton and West Acton, both on the 5th November 1923. The Central London's terminus at Ealing Broadway was conveniently sited between that of the District line and the Great Western Railway's main-line station, and all three stations were linked for easy passenger interchange. The Central London quickly became popular with Ealing people, as it provided a quicker, more direct, route to the heart of the West End and the City than that provided by the District line.

In 1937 a pair of separate tracks was provided for the Great Western Railway to avoid increasing congestion. Some Great Western local trains – often composed of saloon trailers and tank engines – also called at the three Acton stations, coming off the West London Railway. Work on the additional pair of lines was completed in 1938.

The London Passenger Transport Board's New Works Plan provided for a long extension of the Central line beside the Great Western Railway's High Wycombe line as far out as Denham. The Great Western was to build the line, and Central line trains would provide the through service from Essex, where a number of LNER suburban lines were to be electrified and worked by London Transport as part of the Central line.

Work began on the Central line extensions in the late 1930s and, by September 1939, was well advanced at least as far as Greenford. Even beyond, bridges were being widened and sites cleared for stations. One of the earliest known occasions of bulldozers being used in Britain was in 1938–39 for the clearance of the vast site for the Ruislip Central line depot. The increasing shortage of manpower and materials brought any further work

on the extensions to a final halt in about 1941. In fact it was not possible to open Greenford Central line station until 1947 – two years after the end of the Second World War – and the opening of West Ruislip Central line station did not take place until 1948.

However, the continuation of the line to Denham was abandoned. Suburban development began along the line in the mid-1930s in anticipation of the Underground extensions. But the sites of the new stations and their Great Western Railway halt predecessors never attracted the shopping centres so typical of the other lines. The districts near the line tended to be light industrial in nature. The houses were mainly of the terraced type seen in the Hounslow area. Ruislip Gardens estate, west of West End Road, was started in 1934.

The Davis estate at South Ruislip (Dudley Drive/Acol Crescent), dates from 1937. The edges of the vast Manor Homes estate were within easy walking distance of the line. H P Taylor's Deane Park estate got under way at South Ruislip (an area formerly known as Northolt Junction) by the late 1930s. Taylor's houses began along Victoria Road, Queen's Drive and Long Drive, but the estate was not finished until the 1950s.

Some very early developments of small bungalows and chalets had taken place at South Ruislip almost from the opening of the Great Western Railway/Great Central Railway joint line from 1913 onwards. But the area was never really built up with sufficient shops and amenities for many years.

At Denham, in anticipation of the line's arrival, a parade of shops appeared and a few houses, but the proposed suburb was really just an appendage to the then famous Denham Film Studios.

Facing page top **Perivale Great Western Railway halt in 1935. This station had opened on 1st May 1904 amid tranquil meadows below Horsenden Hill. Clifford's Perivale Park houses are being offered at £595 (15/9d per week). Taylor Woodrow were also selling houses in the area at this date.**

Facing page bottom **Northolt – the Great Western halt opened on 1st March 1907. This picture was taken in 1937. Note the new houses under construction on the left in Carr Road. Northolt Central line station opened on 21st November 1948 on the opposite side of Mandeville Road, and the halt was then demolished.**

Although work began on the Central line extension in the late 1930s, the Second World War delayed the arrival of the tube trains until 1947. Greenford – the new station under construction in May 1947. The centre bay platform is for the Great Western shuttle train to Ealing Broadway. The houses on the right are in Greenford Road. The station opened on the 30th June 1947. Greenford is now unique in having an escalator which takes passengers up to the train.

Station Approach, South Ruislip.

South Ruislip was originally called Northolt Junction and was opened in 1908 at a point then described as being close to where 'there are still vast tracks of open country and not a score of houses within a mile'. There were early developments here before 1914 of the 'plotlander' type. Many of these plots of land were not finally built upon until the 1960s. In fact in 1926 a local councillor described the area around the station as a 'higgledy piggledy bungalow town'. These shops are in Station Approach. On the 18th October 1942 an RAF bomber was attempting to land at Northolt Aerodrome, just down the road, when it crashed on the shops. The crew and 21 people were killed.

SOUTH RUISLIP

VICTORIA PARK

Piccadilly Tube to Sth.Harrow Station and Bus 158 passes through Estate, alight at Victoria Road. Good Shops, including multiples a few minutes' walk, schools and other amenities all close at hand. The Central London Railway extension, now under construction, provides a Station right on the Estate.

All Houses are Freehold and free of all Road and Legal charges.

£525-£725
FROM 13/7 WEEKLY
Deposit £25-£30 as in

Bungalows £695, 18/- Weekly. Several types £525, £545, £625, £695, £725. Come and see them all. Really well constructed Houses in healthy surroundings. Large bright airy rooms, latest type fittings and cabinets. The majority semi-detached with large gardens, garage space in most cases.

CLIFFORDS ESTATES

VICTORIA PARK ESTATE, VICTORIA ROAD, SOUTH RUISLIP
'Phone . Byron 3518

ON THE GREEN BELT

30 minutes from Town

NEAR Shops, Schools, Cinemas and 5 Train Services

RUISLIP and ICKENHAM

Only 8 to an acre Surrounded by beautiful wooded country, these individually built, varied-in-type Houses and Bungalows offer construction, finish, fittings and character well above the average. Steel girders. Solid joinery. Fireproof ceilings. No mass production. No straight roads.

FREEHOLD £765 to £995 FROM 18/- WEEKLY

ENGLISH HOUSES LTD.

ICKENHAM: Derwent Avenue, Swakeleys Road (Ruislip 4224)

Coupon for illustrated booklet

Name ....

Address ....

.... W.M.G. 4/3/39

Press adverts for new housing. The Cliffords advert refers to 'The Central London railway extension, now under construction' while that for English Houses speaks of the 'Green Belt' that was to make West Ruislip a somewhat quieter outpost of the Central line than had been expected.

103

Left **Ruislip Gardens – the original Great Western halt** photographed in 1937 showing the down platform. The Central line station now occupies the land seen here. This halt opened on 9th July 1934 to serve the ever-spreading nearby housing estates, which included the southern part of the vast Ruislip Manor estate. Taylor Woodrow were also building off West End Road. Here bungalows and houses were for sale from £496 to £675. Some of the houses included Aztec style fireplaces with built-in wireless sets.

Right **West Ruislip: Great Central Parade, 1928.** Just beyond the shops is the entrance to The Greenway, built from 1925 onwards. On the left of the picture is the station boundary fence, later removed for road widening in conjunction with the Central line in 1939, although work was not finally to be completed until the 1950s after the Central line had opened.

Below left **Construction work on the new Ruislip Gardens station** in August 1939. Shortly afterwards all work on the extension ceased, until 1947. But not everybody was excited at the prospect of the new tube trains. A letter in the local press in 1938 feared that the fields would all soon be turned into a muddy replica of Ruislip Manor or Rayners Lane.

Below **Ickenham village** remained rural until the early 1930s. This picture was taken by the pond and ornamental pump in 1938. Just to the right of the pump at Church Farm are the elaborate hoardings announcing Dunster Richardson's Milton Court estate. In 1939 a parade of shops went up on this site, although they were not fully occupied until after the Second World War.

The Pond and Pump, Ickenham.

The Green Belt.

As early as 1932, the Middlesex County Council had paid £226,000 towards the cost of buying a portion of the countryside near Hendon for Green Belt. Sir Montague Barlow's Royal Commission on the growth of London (1938) laid the foundations of the Green Belt idea. Despite the London Passenger Transport Board's New Works Programme 1935–40, with the grandiose schemes for Northern line expansion to Elstree and Central line expansion west to Denham and east to Ongar, the days were coming to an end for suburbia's insatiable appetite.

It was after the Second World War that the Green Belt Plan was realised. Based on the Abercrombie Greater London Development Plan, the final curb on expansion into the countryside came into effect with the Town & Country Planning Act 1947.

But there were other curbs on the development of Underground suburbs by 1938. Builders were indeed anticipating the arrival of the Central line to Ruislip and Denham, and some building was taking place at Greenford, Northolt and South Ruislip. The first parades of shops went up at Denham near the Film Studios; but there was a reluctance to start really big estates. The very last estates were advertised in the *Evening News* of 26th August 1939. An accompanying feature announced 'the pick of the safety zones' for new houses outside the central and southern areas of London.

Many of the empty houses and flats were quickly occupied in 1940 by those people who feared bombing as well as those who had been 'bombed out'. The unexpected sirens of Sunday, the 3rd September 1939 sounded the end of the Underground suburbs.

In the last 12 months, 15,000 families moved out of Central London and set up 15,000 new homes in the suburbs

 LONDON TRANSPORT MEANS HEALTHIER HOMES

Left **By the late 1930s much of the Middlesex countryside had already been successfully covered by concrete and bricks. It was by now fairly common for even semi-detached houses to have garages (usually at extra cost). The fields near the house in this view were saved by the coming of the Second World War and, afterwards, by the Green Belt Act. Francis Jackson began at Ickenham what had been intended to be another estate that would have included shops and a cinema south of the station.**

Right **By the end of the 1930s the pace of suburban development was slackening. The pretty village of Denham had been in the Underground's sights but the Central line, in the event, got no further than West Ruislip.**

Above **Press advert from 1938.**

Below **Central line destination plate prepared for the line's extension to Denham as part of a plan drawn up in 1935.**

7
POSTSCRIPT

With the outbreak of the Second World War, the construction of new houses came to a stop and, indeed, there was not the manpower or materials to spare for this industry. Likewise, both young and unmarried men and husbands were being called up to serve their country, so that the public lost the urge to buy new homes. 'The bomber will get through', it was said, 'and everything could be lost in a flash'. It had been much the same at the outbreak of the First World War, although the air threat did not materialise to such a devastating extent. Between these two terrible world events, London's green countryside changed almost overnight into a vast area of houses stretching out in all directions.

Following the peak years of expansion between 1933–36, there was a decline, so that by 1939 the larger builders were already running out of land. The grand plans of extending the Northern line into Hertfordshire, bringing the delights of semi-detached living, shopping parades and cinemas, came to an end in 1940. By 1938 men and materials were being switched to constructing airfields, army camps, public air raid shelters and Government factories.

Another factor was that the market for new houses had declined by 1939. Amazingly, most housing projects seem to have been completed by the outbreak of War and there were few instances of empty shells awaiting completion.

But there were other factors behind the decline in suburban growth. The urge to seek fresh air and green spaces became less important, as healthier living as well as private motoring became more commonplace. As early as 1937 the number of travellers up to central London for entertainment was in decline as homes became more comfortable and local entertainment was established.

After 1945 the shortage of building materials plus Government restrictions on private development gave priority to Council housing projects and New Town development. But most important of all was the London Green Belt which put a stop to the expanding girth of giant London.

In recent times more wealthy commuters who thought that the edge of civilisation was at Edgware or Moor Park now come into London from as far as Peterborough and even Bristol. Today, suburbs are criss-crossed by motorways, shopping malls and entertainment and leisure complexes.

The suburban shopping parades, once the domain of the butcher, baker and greengrocer, are in decline. They are now replaced by discount stores, ethnic restaurants and travel agencies, whilst the remaining cinema buildings are now nightclubs, health clubs or have been converted into multi-screen operations. The red brick new-Tudor public houses, once smoking male preserves, have now been converted into smart cafe-bars for all the family. Even the social structure of the suburb has changed. On the tube to central London, Mr John Brown in his grey suit is more likely to be sitting beside Ms Jones in her grey suit and her Walkman.

There will always be a demand for the Underground to serve the suburbs, provided the Underground itself is clean and efficient, if not speedy, not just to take commuters into London but to take commuters out to the newer office developments in outer London, such as Uxbridge.

Our new century may well see the older Underground suburbs redeveloped with low rise apartments and smaller houses around closes and courtyards, but the Underground suburb will still be with us.

INDEX

BIBLIOGRAPHY AND SOURCES

Alan A Jackson has been of particular help in the writing of this book and reference has been made to four of his works:

London's Metropolitan Railway – David & Charles 1986
Rails Through the Clay (Desmond F Croome co-author) – 2nd edition Capital Transport 1993
Semi-Detached London – 2nd edition Wild Swan 1991
London's Local Railways – 2nd edition Capital Transport 1999

Another useful reference was the History of London Transport Volume 2 by TC Barker and Michael Robbins – Allen & Unwin 1974

Local Archives

Grange Museum, London Borough of Brent
Harrow Reference Library
Hillingdon Archives, Uxbridge Reference Library

Local Newspapers

Middlesex Advertiser and Gazette
Middlesex County Times
Harrow Observer

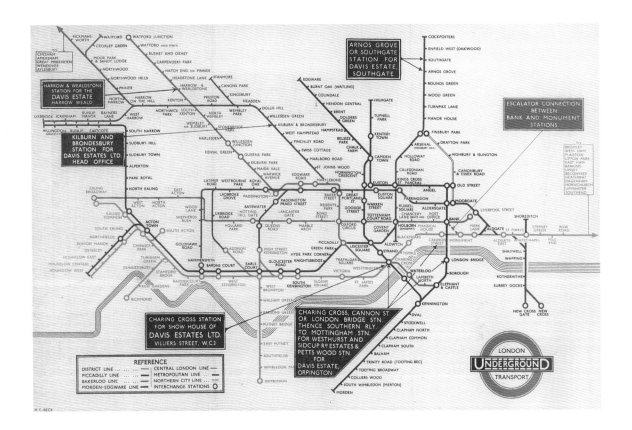